Hawthorns and Medlars

Hawthorns and Medlars

James B. Phipps

with Robert J. O'Kennon and Ron W. Lance

TIMBER PRESS

Portland • Cambridge

ROYAL HORTICULTURAL SOCIETY

Published in 2003 by
Timber Press, Inc.   Timber Press
The Haseltine Building   2 Station Road
133 S.W. Second Avenue, Suite 450   Swavesey
Portland, Oregon 97204, U.S.A.   Cambridge CB4 5QJ, U.K.

Printed through Colorcraft Ltd., Hong Kong

Library of Congress Cataloging-in-Publication Data

Phipps, J. B. (James Bird), 1934–
    Hawthorns and medlars / James B. Phipps with Robert J. O'Kennon and Ron W. Lance.
        p.   cm.—(Royal Horticultural Society plant collector guide)
    Includes bibliographical references (p.   ).
    ISBN 0-88192-591-8
    1. Hawthorns. 2. Medlars (Plants) I. O'Kennon, Bob, 1942– II. Lance, Ron. III. Title.
        IV. Series.

    QK495.R78P47 2003
    583'.73—dc21
                                                                    2003048407

A catalog record for this book is also available from the British Library.

Contents

5

PART TWO: THE CAST OF CHARACTERS

Color plates follow page 64

Preface and Acknowledgments

W HEN TIMBER PRESS approached me about writing this book, I was happy to agree. I have been studying the systematics of hawthorns and medlars for more than 25 years, which has led to an extensive field knowledge of the two genera. For much of this period I have also been director of a small arboretum, generated my own living research collection of nearly 300 hawthorn plants, cultivated some hawthorns and both medlars in my own garden, and seen many in prestigious arboreta of the Western world. This background has given me first-hand experience of most of what I write about here. This work is aimed at horticulturists and plantspeople and is in no sense a monographic treatment, which is under preparation as a separate work. I believe that this is the first book devoted exclusively to medlars and hawthorns.

Chief among those who made this work possible are my co-authors Robert O'Kennon and Ron Lance. These gentlemen, two of the finest field botanists I have encountered, share a love of hawthorns and have accompanied me on field trips. The value of these associations is more than is immediately obvious, for a single person cannot alone, even in 25 years, gain an adequately complete knowledge of so large and wide-ranging a group of plants.

Bob is a retired commercial pilot whose passion for botany has led to his becoming vice-chair of the Botanical Research Institute of Texas in Fort Worth. He is co-author of the new *Shinner's Illustrated Flora of Texas* (with George Diggs and Barney Lipscomb). An excellent photographer and warm friend, he has regularly accompanied me in the field since our first meeting in 1988 and has described nine hawthorns with me. I thank him for his friendship, energy in the field, generous supply of photographs, and for going beyond the call of duty in hunting down hawthorns alone when necessary.

Ron is nursery curator of Chimney Rock Nursery in western North Carolina, where he produces woody plants for the trade. He developed an exceptional knowledge of the woody flora of the southeastern United States during 22 years of employment with the state of North Carolina. A fine artist and botanical photographer, he has written and illustrated several books on hawthorns and is preparing a comprehensive winter guide to southeastern woody plants. He has done significant fieldwork with the other two authors and has rescued *Crataegus harbisonii* from extinction.

Bob and Ron, you have my heartfelt thanks.

Next comes my wife, Sheila, who looks after our property during my numerous *Crataegological* absences and comes on the occasional field trip. She has typed most of the manuscript for this book and proofed many other manuscripts of mine. She is the one upon whose work this book ultimately significantly depends and she has been a constant source of support. We are not far from providing her with a more permanent memento.

Next, there are persons in the United Kingdom who provided invaluable *pieds-à-terre* for visits to the famous arboreta and libraries at Edinburgh and Kew and generally quarterbacked my travel arrangements over the pond from their scattered homes. These are Tony (A. D.) Househam of Esher, Surrey, and his dear departed wife, Meg; my sisters Elva Phipps of Harborne, Birmingham, and Barbara Tromans of Whitton, Shropshire, as well as Philip and Eira Smith of Balerno, near Edinburgh.

Direct help in locating critical hawthorns was also provided by Alan Harris when deputy warden of Saltwells Nature Reserve, West Midlands, and by Mark Bridger, in charge of the South Arboretum at the Royal Botanic Gardens, Kew. Laura Hastings, librarian of the Economic Botany Unit, Kew, was instrumental in leading me through the unfamiliar literature on the medicinal uses of hawthorns. The Missouri Botanical Garden, St. Louis, principally through interaction with George Yatskievych, has also provided the wherewithal to significantly increase my understanding of hawthorns.

In addition to the above who get special mention, numerous botanists have helped me locate hawthorns or aided my understanding of them, not least a string of excellent graduate students, now professional botanists themselves. To everyone who has helped me understand hawthorns and medlars, I offer my sincere thanks.

Introduction

THIS BOOK is about hawthorns (*Crataegus*) and medlars (*Mespilus*). These two genera are shrubby, Northern Hemisphere members of the rose family, Rosaceae. They are so closely related that they were often confused well into the 19th century. *Crataegus* is very large for a genus of temperate woody plants, comprising perhaps 140 species widespread through the north temperate regions, about half of which are mentioned here. Many hawthorns are, or could be, excellent ornamentals and their sheer number warrants a book. By contrast, the merely two medlar species are most conveniently treated in a book with the hawthorns. A subsidiary objective of this book is to consider why relatively few hawthorns are in general cultivation and to suggest remedies to this problem.

This book is arranged to balance general knowledge about hawthorns (part one, chapters 1–5) with an account of the most important kinds for ornamental horticulture (part two, chapters 6–8). Appendices, a glossary, and a bibliography round out the treatment.

Part one starts by considering the lore of hawthorns (chapter 1) which readily attracts our interest. In northern Europe, the Queen of the May is the queen of the hawthorns, especially *Crataegus monogyna*, while the Holy Thorn of Somerset is a tale in itself. Chapter 2 treats the structure of the hawthorn plant to help us understand its biology. The significant role of hawthorns in the natural landscape is considered in sections on ecology and conservation. Unfortunately, this role is generally inadequately appreciated, with foresters being primarily interested in tall forest trees with straight boles to produce high-quality timber, and farmers interested in clear grassy pastures and weedless ploughed land so that components of scrubby vegetation tend to be overlooked as unimportant. The very important practical value of hawthorns and medlars is, of course, implicit in this book and includes pomology, food, ornamental horticulture, agricultural husbandry, medicine, and turnery—all of which are discussed in chapter 3. The cultivation and propagation of these plants, as well as the pests and diseases they may encounter, are treated in chapter 4, where I try to be frank so that readers understand problems that may be associated with the cultivation of some hawthorns. By contrast, chapter 5 proposes solutions: there is indeed a potential bonanza of hawthorns if plant breeders were to work on improving plant resistance to disease, fruit quality in edible and potentially edible forms, and fruiting characteristics of ornamental hawthorns; on reducing suckering in some cases; or on widening the range of flower color.

Part two begins with a discussion of the classification of hawthorns and medlars and includes information on how to approach their identification confidently (chapter 6). Chapters 7 and 8 detail a considerable selection of the kinds of wild hawthorns and medlars, including many beautiful species rarely, if ever, cultivated outside botanic gardens and arboreta. These chapters also deal with the main horticultural variants. It is hoped that a knowledge of those types of hawthorn beyond the commonly cultivated ones may spur an interest in their cultivation.

PART ONE
General

CHAPTER *1*

Hawthorns and Medlars
in Folklore

Lore refers to the folk customs and beliefs of traditional societies. In this sense "lore" is separate from true practical knowledge, such as for food and medicine, which are discussed in chapter 3 and which, if traditional, are covered under ethnobotany. Folklore also is separate from representational art. Hawthorns, and to a lesser extent medlars, have been represented numerous times in bas-relief on stone or wood (for example, see Mabey 1996) and in painting, and the hawthorn was significant enough that Henry VIII chose it as his personal emblem for the Field of the Cloth of Gold (Weir 2001). In more modern times the state of Missouri has adopted *Crataegus mollis* (downy haw) as the state flower.

Human beings and their ancestors have had a long, continuous and intimate association with plants and use them for every conceivable purpose, including food, fiber, fuel, construction, medicine, flavoring, and ornament. But, as well as understanding the more obviously utilitarian functions of plants, traditional societies have developed a lore about many of them, and hawthorns and medlars are no exception. Much of this lore is sheer superstition, but some of it is grounded in fact, and some of it entered into the rituals of the society concerned.

My knowledge of the literature on hawthorn and medlar lore is that of northwestern Europe, especially Britain and France, but it is certain that all other societies in which hawthorns or medlars are a significant part of the landscape or ecosystem have their own lore about these plants. There is, indeed, a huge folklore on hawthorns and medlars indigenous to all countries where these plants grow naturally or have been traditionally cultivated, which could warrant a book of its own by a person prepared to conduct the research. I give here merely a sampling.

13

According to Vickery (1995), who made extensive surveys via the Folklore Society, hawthorn flowers were mentioned in 23.5 percent of "unlucky" items, more than twice the number recorded for lilac, the next most-feared plant. How seriously the respondents "fear" the hawthorn is a matter for psychological analysis since actual morbidity directly associated with hawthorns, either by incidental infection after pricking oneself on their thorns or by eating very large and toxic amounts of fruit or foliage, must be very low, although a moderate amount of minor injury due to scratching would be familiar to rural people. In particular it was considered unlucky to bring hawthorn blossom into the house. Such a view could derive from a belief that Christ's crown of thorns was made from *Crataegus* (not likely, but not impossible), or from the rather heavy aminiferous smell of the blossom, which many actually do find unpleasant when too strong, and which is said to resemble the aroma of death.

Interestingly, a contrary view can be found in Italy, France, and other traditionally Catholic countries where hawthorns, as May-flowers, are Mary's flowers, and therefore worthy of special affection. It was thought during penal times in Protestant countries that if Catholics brought those flowers to their own doors in May, this would identify them and bring bad luck. Elsewhere people brought into their houses a fully flowering hawthorn branch on old May-day (that is, prior to the Gregorian calendar). This custom indicated a very early spring and was therefore auspicious for agriculture as heralding a long growing season. In Ireland, hawthorn was used to protect the household from evil on May-day.

Friend (1884) notes how May-flowers were used for adorning houses and churches and quotes Edmund Spenser's *Shepherd's Calendar*:

> Youth's folk now flocken everywhere
> To gather May-baskets and smelling breere;
> and home they hasten the posts to dight,
> and all the kirk-pillars ere day-light
> with hawthorne buds and Sweet Eglantine
> and girlands of Roses and Sops-in-wine
> And forth goth all the court both most and leste,
> to fetch the flouris fresh, and branch and blome,
> and namely hawthorn brought both page and grome,
> with fresh garlandis, party blew and white,
> and than rejoysin in there grete delight.

The custom of going out before dawn on May-day lingered in Cornwall until at least "not long ago" (Friend 1884). It is reported that on May-day Eve young people assembled at the inn and waited until the clock struck twelve midnight. They then walked around and eventually went off in search of May, returning between five and six A.M. They decked certain houses and porches with elm, sycamore, and hawthorn. The custom came to be called dipping-day because the young people would then attempt to splash with water people from houses not protected by Mayflowers.

Many other examples of "good" or "bad" properties of hawthorn abound, but in my opinion all these "values" of hawthorn for good or ill have their origin in the mind. Nevertheless, they are of great interest to the sociologist in analyzing the beliefs and dynamics of traditional rural societies. Such stories should always be treated with respect as possibly being an inadvertent cover for some not-understood beneficent or maleficent phenomenon.

One of the most interesting examples of hawthorn lore concerns the Holy Thorn of Glastonbury, which has a tradition centuries old. In the picturesque little town of Glastonbury, in the county of Somerset, in the southwest of England, are several trees of the Holy Thorn (*Crataegus monogyna* 'Biflora'). This form of the common European hawthorn has the unusual characteristic of flowering twice (hence 'Biflora'), the first time being around Christmas and New Year (Plate 1) and the second being at the typical time in spring, about May. It also has at least some green foliage throughout the winter. The holy thorns now existing in Glastonbury are lineal descendants of a tree(s) associated with the town that have been reproduced by grafting over the centuries (Plate 2).

Legend has it that Saint Joseph of Arimathea, a disciple of Christ, reached the Glastonbury area of Somerset in the first century of this era and struck his holy staff of hawthorn into the ground, and that it miraculously sprouted. According to this legend, the saint was the first person to introduce Christianity to what would later be called England, A.D. 36. Unfortunately, every aspect of this story is devoid of documentation and it resembles the numerous similar miracles of early saints that developed in medieval times; however, the grain of truth in it could be that the Holy Thorn of Glastonbury did have its origin in a Mediterranean area of mild winters where such winter flowering occasionally occurs naturally, according to the Danish botanist Knud Christensen (1992).

Glastonbury is a place rich in legend and myth and, according to Dunning (1976), it also has a special place in the Arthurian legend, for King Arthur and his knights spent their time [there] in search of the Holy Grail; Glastonbury is the Isle of Avalon to which the king was "borne away for the healing of his wounds," and Pomparles, the Bridge Perilous, where the King threw his sword Excalibur into the water and an arm came out to receive it, is the bridge crossing the River Brue between Glastonbury and Street.

Furthermore, Glastonbury was the place where the bodies of Arthur and Guinevere were discovered, buried between two mysterious pyramids near the abbey with an inscription that "proved" Glastonbury to be Avalon. Certainly in 1191 the monks of Glastonbury opened the "tomb of Arthur" to public view (and subscription).

Documentation available to us today of the existence of Glastonbury holy thorns (Vickery 1979) commences with an anonymous poem of 1520 about three such trees on Wearyall Hill, Glastonbury. These trees

> Do burge and bere grene leaves at Christmas
> As fresihe as other in May when ye nightingale
> Wrestes out her notes musycall as pure glass.

Thereafter, there are regular references in the 16th century, for instance, by W. Turner (1562) and J. Gerard (1597). It is fairly clear that the tradition was well established at this time. According to the folklorist C. Hole (1976), local tradition states that a miraculous tree was planted at Appleton in the county of Cheshire in 1125 and that this was an offshoot of the Glastonbury thorn. It is also worth noting that only about 16 kilometers from Glastonbury is the village of Hallatrow, whose name is a corruption of the Saxon *Helgetrev* or Holy Tree. Helgetrev already existed in 1087 as it is mentioned in the Domesday Book. Is it not possible that the holy tree of Helgetrev was a twice-flowering hawthorn and that, after its remarkable and perhaps miraculous winter-flowering characteristics had been fully appreciated and assessed, it was moved to Glastonbury Abbey? If so, the Glastonbury thorn is an English, not a Mediterranean, hawthorn. Indeed, a wild twice-flowering *Crataegus monogyna* has been found by Alan Harris in the English West Midlands, at Saltwells Nature Reserve, Dudley (Plate 3), which strengthens the possibility for English origin.

In modern times the tradition of the Holy Thorn is still carried on. Every mid-December (at varying dates) a short service is conducted by the vicar of Glastonbury outside his parish church of St. John the Baptist at which children from the local schools assemble and sing a short carol composed for the occasion. The mayor and town leaders in their official regalia are also present, while the youngest schoolchild present ascends a stepladder, cuts pieces of flowering Glastonbury thorn (Plate 4), and places them in a basket to be dispatched as a gift to the Queen. This short but colorful ceremony is well worth attending by visitors to the area.

In view of the loss of the abbey records during the Reformation, it is doubtful, therefore, if archival research will uncover much more than is already known about the origins and early history of the Holy Thorn of Glastonbury; however, modern science could lend a hand. Genetic probing should be able to establish whether the Glastonbury thorn is a mutation of normal local Somersetshire hawthorns or is related to a Mediterranean form of *Crataegus monogyna*. Such research is technically very sophisticated and could be expensive (especially given the sampling logistics needed). Furthermore, relatively few are equipped or funded to do it. The mystery of the Glastonbury thorns may remain for a considerable time.

The common medlar is and has been far more abundant in France than in England, and it is there that Rolland (1904) collected so many folkloric references to it. Some involve Satan, others are riddles or allusions to the plant's lack of value. For instance,

> The medlar presents a remarkable phenomenon towards the month of May, in which it is believed, by superstitious people, that the devil comes out to beat the tree with a long pole and mutilate the young buds, thus destroying the harvest of those who have forgotten to hallow the eve of 1 May (C. E. Royer).

Similarly, "On 1 May one should shake holy water at the bottom of the medlar-tree if one doesn't want the devil to come and cut the braches" (Dottin) and "The wands of sorcerers are made from branches of medlar cut on the night of St. John at the moment of the appearance of the first rays of the sun" (Dottin). A French riddle states: *Quel est le fruit qui est comme l'église, qui a St. Pierre?* (What fruit is like a church that has St. Peter?). The answer, *cinq pierres* (five stones), is a word play referring to the fruit of medlar. One French saying claims that *Cité de Neflier* (Medlar City) equals *Ville de rien* (Nothing City). Another refers to the very crooked branches of medlars: *Aussi droit que branche d'vieil mellier* (As straight as the branch of an old medlar).

A great deal of French lore simply affirms the well understood fact that medlar fruit must be over-ripe (bletted) before it's of any value. The following poem was included in a collection of oral literature of lower Normandy compiled by J. Fleury (translation by M.-B. Hamel, University of Caen, France):

À la Saint-Michiei
On met les mêles à blhikiéy;
À la Toussaint
Ils devent être blheques à tout le mains.

At Michaelmas [St. Michael's Day, 29 September]
One puts the medlars out to blet;
By All Saints' Day [1 November], at the very latest,
They should be bletted.

In case there's any confusion, I'll end by *À la Saint-Simon, le fruit du meslier est bon* (At the feast of St. Simon [28 October] the fruit of the medlar is good).

CHAPTER 2

Natural History and Conservation, Structure and Reproductive Biology

To UNDERSTAND hawthorns and medlars, it is important to learn about their natural history, structure, and reproductive biology. Not only will this help with care and appreciation, but it also will assist readers without a botanical background and may encourage some to look into relevant useful technical literature.

Hawthorns may be very common and consequently exert a profound ecological effect. For this reason, and simply to understand them better, it is interesting to study their ecology. In this section we discuss habitat and most obvious adaptations that hawthorns have made to their habitat. A short section on conservation follows. Next, the detailed structure of the hawthorn and medlar plant is an essential backdrop to their biology, classification, and identification. Aspects of floral and fruit biology are considered in the last section. Medlars have a similar biology and structure to hawthorns and are not considered separately.

ECOLOGY

Hawthorns are mostly medium-sized to large shrubs or small trees that range widely throughout the north temperate zone. They may occur as scattered individuals, in small groups, or in thickets, and where common, they have a great impact on the environment. Hawthorn thickets are a superb home to smaller and medium-sized wildlife—a rich assortment of mammals, birds, reptiles, insects, and other forms of life. Nesting sites abound and thorny protection is everywhere. In spring, at mass flowering, the air is alive with thousands of bees, flies, and other insects. In autumn, where common, the great crop of hawthorn fruit attracts many birds, rodents, and larger animals. The fruit crops of hawthorn can be immense in good years and constitute part of their considerable impact on the natural environment. In some regions hawthorns play a major role in the natural succession from grassland to woodland and can be extremely important as agents of erosion control when they are common.

REGION OF OCCURRENCE. The natural home for hawthorns is the entire temperate Northern Hemisphere so long as it is not too dry (temperate desert) or too cold (high montane or boreal forest). The southern boundary goes nearly to the southern edge of the temperate zone. No *Crataegus* species are native in the Southern Hemisphere, but *C. monogyna* is widely naturalized there and other species occasionally so.

Within the temperate zone, three principal subzones are amenable to hawthorns and medlars: first, the adequate summer rainfall (75–150 cm per year) subzone as manifested in nature by temperate deciduous forest, and nowadays with plentiful agriculture; second, a dryish subzone, with low summer rainfall (38–62 cm per year) and cold winters, as exemplified by natural grasslands (steppes, prairies); and third, a winter rainfall subzone as exemplified by Mediterranean Europe and North Africa extending to Afghanistan and the mountains of Kazakhstan.

Each of these subzones hosts about a third of the hawthorn species. Hawthorns of the first subzone are mesophytes, generally liking open conditions in the North and light forest shade in the South. Hawthorns of the second subzone may also be somewhat mesophytic, then principally occurring along the smaller, often intermittent, watercourses or ditches. Hawthorns of the last subzone are the most xeromorphic and often the most thorny, occurring in maquis and other thorny scrub.

The two medlar species, one of the south-central United States, the other of areas around the southern Black Sea and the southern Caspian Sea, both fit within the main areas of hawthorn distribution.

HABITAT AND ADAPTATIONS TO HABITAT. While most hawthorns are mesophytes of sites that get lots of light, a number tolerate, and a few like, flooding of the root zone. Good examples of this last category are *Crataegus nigra* of the Danubian floodplain and the May-haws (*Crataegus* series *Aestivales*) of the southeastern United States, which normally grow in sinkholes or along rivers. Contrasted with this, several *Crataegus* species are relative xeromorphs at the other end of the moisture spectrum. Examples of this group include all members of series *Lacrimatae*, species of dry, often burnt, usually sandy sites of the pine flats of the southeastern United States. Further examples of xeromorphy are found in the gray-leaved members of series *Tanacetifoliae* and *Orientales*, and some members of series *Crataegus* of the southern European and west Asian maquis.

Thorniness is an important defense against browsing and reduces its intensity. This feature becomes more accentuated in drier regions or under high grazing intensity. A pictorial example is shown in the bizarre topiarized forms of hawthorns in high-elevation cattle pastures in North Carolina (Plate 5). Thorniness is important for plant species such as hawthorns, which are both palatable when soft and nontoxic.

SUCCESSION AND CHANGES IN ABUNDANCE. Hawthorns don't, so far as we know, live a long while, a characteristic of shrubs in general. In the northern part of the eastern United States eventual shading out by deciduous trees spells the demise of hawthorns in the natural scheme of things so that 25–50 years would be a usual maximum age for many. Little research has been done on oldest trees of hawthorn, but about 100 years of slow growth would seem to be at the extreme high end in all probability.

Hawthorn abundance in the wild is not necessarily constant. Because of the somewhat weedy and opportunistic nature of many hawthorns, it appears that they have become more common in many regions of human settlement than would have been the case in nature. Not all, human activities, however, are beneficial to hawthorns. Too intensive a use of land, whether agricultural or industrial, eliminates them. Generally, if most deciduous woodland has been cleared, hawthorns are rare—the forest edge is an important survival zone. Likewise the introduction of exotic competition is apparently very serious in some cases. In North America the Asiatic shrub *Lonicera maackii* has colonized immense areas in a region centered in Kentucky. Unfortunately, its competitive exclusion of native plants has still not been thoroughly investigated and the precise effects on hawthorns are not documented. In similar latitudes and longitudes another honeysuckle, the vine *L. japonica*, has been let loose. It effectively out-competes hawthorns in woodland edge habitats in an immense area centered perhaps on Tennessee. Favored hawthorn colonization sites—fence lines and woodland edges—are no longer tenable. *Lonicera japonica* is now considered one of the most important weed species on state and federal lands in the United States (Schweitzer and Larson 1999). These two cases constitute object lessons of the damaging effects on native flora when exotics are introduced, an issue that most horticulturists have all too little awareness of. Eventually, legislation will ban commerce in invasive exotics.

A further example of the diminution of hawthorn populations also comes from the same general region as the last two and is related to fire-suppression, beloved by humans but anathema to much wildlife. In many areas fire-suppression has been greatly increased in recent decades so that serious fires are now a much less frequent occurrence in states like Missouri, for instance, a state naturally well-wooded but with extensive glades on the thinner, more rocky soils. Glades often support red-cedar, *Juniperus virginiana*, which is the alternate host of the damaging cedar-hawthorn rust or cedar-apple rust, *Gymnosporangium*. Regular fire decimates red cedar and also opens up the habitat for hawthorns, which then have little competition from the juniper and a concomitantly lessened threat from *Gymnosporangium*. Ecosystems can have complex feedback mechanisms. Missouri is typical of the mid-latitudes of the eastern half of the United States in that hawthorns are, apparently, much less numerous now than in, say, the period 1900–1930. Indeed, in Missouri, some species previously known can no longer be found, and some, once common, are reduced to tiny remnant populations.

COLONIZATION. The issue of colonization of new sites is central to hawthorn survival. Since the ecological status of many sites is in a state of flux, in the deciduous forest areas hawthorn populations need to be mobile, a need exacerbated by their relatively short life-span. This is why frugivore dispersers are so important, although little is known with precision on this topic relative to hawthorns. In drier areas where hawthorns generally remain attached to watercourses and shading out by trees is less severe, the need for great mobility may be lessened somewhat. Here we need only add that the pyrene requires a suitable site to germinate and that germination in colder latitudes (zone 7 and lower) is usually in the second spring while in warmer latitudes (zone 8 and higher) it is in the first.

CONSERVATION

Many hawthorns have become rare, for a variety of reasons noted earlier in the chapter. These include improved fire-suppression, competition with exotics, highly intensive human exploitation of land, and return of farmland to forest. Thus, hawthorns have become much scarcer than they were 100 years ago in places like New England as hill farming has gradually given way to woodland, a reversal of the sequence following settlement, and due to economics. As woodland replaces farmland and becomes denser in many parts of New England, few, or no, hawthorns survive reproductively below the new forest canopy and suitable woodland gap habitat is progressively eliminated. Furthermore, where hawthorns are not used for hedges, farmers see little value in these bushes and consider them worthless competitors—veritable weeds to be grumbled about or grubbed out.

For all these reasons, hawthorn populations have declined substantially in some areas and a number of species of hawthorn, as well as *Mespilus canescens*, are now very rare. A few examples of very rare hawthorns are *Crataegus fecunda*, *C. flava*, *C. lepida*, *C. nitida*, *C. padifolia*, *C. thermopygea*, *C. vailiae*, and *C. warneri*. Indeed some of these species have not been seen for more than 50 years and are likely lost. So there is a serious case for hawthorn conservation, and this is most urgent in anthropogenic habitats where conservation is practiced least. Some hawthorns really need a friend—you may be that person.

STRUCTURE

The larger hawthorns are usually small trees, that is, they are single-trunked and often bare of branches at the base. They may also be bushes, on account of being smaller, or multitrunked, or irregularly trunked, or branched to the ground. Both medlar species are multistemmed bushes. Some authors provide a rigid distinction between bushes and trees, but the truth is that one grades into the other. Some hawthorns have suckering roots that send up stems away from the main trunk, eventually forming small colonies. Heights of up to 15 m have been recorded in the tallest North American species (for example, *Crataegus mollis* in Michigan and *C. okennonii* in British Columbia), but at most perhaps only one in 10,000 reach this size. Substantial trees (more than 9 m tall) may also occur in *C. brachyacantha*, *C. coccinea*, *C. hupehensis*, *C. marshallii*, *C. monogyna*, *C. viridis*, and probably some other species. There are also very small hawthorns, such as *C. lepida*, which can flower at 30 cm tall and may only reach 1 m!

THORNS. Formidable branched (compound) thorns may be present on the trunk and major branches. These are the defensive weapons that keep cattle and deer at bay, and they will have the same effect on you. The smaller branches and twigs generally possess plentiful unbranched thorns which are of characteristic color and which form at 2–3 years old. The twigs are of equal interest and, as they get older, change also; pubescence is lost, and color turns from that of the extension shoot of the season to that of the 1- and then the 2-year-old shoot, after which it stabilizes. Understanding these changes is helpful in identification.

BRANCHES. The branching system of *Crataegus* is characteristic, the plant putting forth both extension or long shoots, which are at the tips of twigs and increase the size of the plant, and short or spur shoots, which are lateral to the above and may grow as little as 1–2 mm in a season. Only the short shoots bear flowers, followed by fruits. Each short shoot bears a rosette of leaves at the end. This efficient division into long and short shoots is quite common in woody plants, being wide-

spread in the rose family and also occurring in many conifers and their allies, notably pines and gingko.

BARK. After a number of years a mature bark develops on the trunk and larger
branches; the patterns and color of this, too, may be helpful in identification. The
bark of mature hawthorn trunks is usually exfoliating. The most common type
breaks into somewhat checkered longitudinal patterns of pale gray-brown alter-
nating with the more recently exposed deeper orange-brown underbark. In these
barks the surface texture of the small flat exfoliating pieces is slightly rough. A
similar type breaking up into larger units is found in some Chinese species. At the
extreme of exfoliation large smooth areas flake off providing beautiful patterning
reminiscent of the lacebark pine; *Crataegus marshallii* and *C. spathulata* are examples. A few hawthorns (for example, series *Lacrimatae* and *Pulcherrimae*) possess
deeply corrugated bark. In at least one species (*C. phippsii*) the bark peels off in
long strips.

FOLIAGE. Leaves of *Crataegus* and *Mespilus* are of various shapes but are typically elliptic to ovate, though sometimes more triangular. The margins are always
toothed, and the teeth may be sharp and strong or very small and blunt. In addition,
the leaves of some species may be deeply lobed, in which case one group of hawthorns possesses veins to the sinuses which are the bays between the lobes. The
overall venation pattern of the leaf is pinnate, that is, there is a principal central vein
and a number of laterals (or secondary veins) springing from either side of the mid-
vein. If the secondary veins reach the margins directly, the venation pattern is
called craspedodromous, otherwise it is called camptodromous. Venation type is
very useful in hawthorn identification. Leaves of hawthorns and medlars vary in
shape even on one tree, sometimes a lot. The variation found in the extension shoots
is much higher than in the short shoots, and therefore, for the purposes of identification, one should normally disregard the extension-shoot leaves and use only typical short-shoot leaves. Moreover, documentation of variation in extension-shoot
foliage is sparse, which is another reason for avoiding it when identifying plants.
The leaf blades are borne on leaf stalks or petioles, and the relative length of petiole to blade is an important helpful identification feature. Gland dots are found on
the petioles and tips of the leaf teeth in many but not all species of hawthorn.

FLOWERS. The flowers of hawthorns and medlars are grouped in small trusses
called inflorescences. The typical inflorescence is flat-topped or slightly convex and
consists of 5–30 flowers, although some species have only one or very few flowers
per inflorescence and occasionally up to 50 are recorded. In nature, the flowers are
practically always white, rather small (usually 10–25 mm in diameter), and of typi-

cal rose family form, except for the relatively unusual inferior ovary which is, however, characteristic of subfamily Maloideae to which hawthorns belong. The carpels are invested by a hypanthium (calyx tube) that lies beneath the sepals and petals. There are five small triangular calyx lobes or sepals, five usually rounded petals with crinkly edges, stamens in multiples of 5 (usually 5, 10, or 20), and 1 to 5 styles leading to hidden carpels. The relative positions of the different floral parts are shown in the vertical section of the flower of the Danubian hawthorn, *Crataegus nigra* (Plate 6).

Fruit. The berrylike fruit of hawthorns and medlars, which begins to develop immediately after pollination, starts off green, swells, and eventually displays one of the numerous attractive colors for which hawthorns are famous—a huge range of reds, through to burgundy, purple, and black in some, and orange, russet, yellow, or pink in others. The common medlar, however, has brown fruit. See details of a typical hawthorn and/or medlar fruit in Plate 6. The fruit (haw) is generally subspherical to broadly ellipsoid and not very big, 6–16 mm diameter being the common range. It may be smooth or hairy, though what the hair is for, no one knows. The apex is open, as the hawthorn hypanthium has never fully closed over the flower, and the opening is usually surrounded by a residual calyx or calyx remnants. Also the curled up and dried remains of the stamens and styles conceal the top of the nutlets. The flesh of the hawthorn and medlar fruits is derived from the hypanthial tissue of the flower and corresponds to the fleshy part of an apple fruit. The very hard nutlets or pyrenes, found in the center of the fruit and themsleves containing two tiny seeds, have developed from the carpels in the flowers and each corresponds to one segment of the core of an apple. Possession of a wide fleshy, edible layer, outside the true ovary, is technically considered to create a pome, the correct name for a hawthorn fruit, rather than a berry. Not surprisingly, the French word for apple, *pomme*, is cognate with pome. The term *haw*, on the other hand, is old English in origin, and while today it refers only to the fruit, it originally meant "hedge," thus the "hawthorn" was a "hedgethorn." Hawthorn fruits are designed for bird or mammal dispersal (see later in this chapter).

Reproductive Biology

The flowering period is among the most critical in the life of the plant. It is of immense importance for it is the first step in the production of seeds. In hawthorns and medlars all flowers open over a short space of time, typically a week. They are thus mass-flowerers, flowering only once per year, typical of so many other spectacular spring-flowering bushes, such as lilac. The flowers are pollinated by a considerable variety of insects, but most preponderantly bees, hover-flies, and some other common flies. The insects are attracted to the flowers by the mass visual effect and the strong odor that combines, in various proportions, a sweet honey scent and a fishy scent, probably aimed at different pollinators. The pollinating insects transfer pollen from the stamens to the stigma.

The breeding system may be sexual, in which case pollen germinates on the stigma and grows down to the egg cell where it effects fertilization. In sexual hawthorns there are self-incompatible species (like apples) in which pollen from the same (self) plant is normally ineffective (this is a device to ensure cross-pollination) and also self-compatible species where own (self) pollen is perfectly effective in securing fertilization, as in peaches. Many hawthorns have a third breeding method called agamospermy, a form of apomixis. In this, there is no union of male and female elements and a substitute for the egg spontaneously develops; it is, therefore, a true parthogenetic or virgin birth. Strangely, in apomictic hawthorns, pollination may be needed to trigger this process, but the pollen will never do its usual job of fertilization. This kind of pollination is called pseudogamous. Whether following apomictic pseudogamy or true fertilization, the ovaries begin to swell and fruit development has commenced.

The flowering season of all hawthorns collectively, if grown in one place, is about six to eight weeks and, given a normal spring, the position of each hawthorn's week of flowering in this sequence will hardly vary. I term hawthorns very early, early, early medium, midseason, late midseason, late, and very late to indicate the position in the local sequence.

FRUITING AND DISPERSAL. Generally by September a ripe-colored fruit has developed which is notable for its usually brilliant color, often red, and edible qualities. This fruit attracts a variety of foragers. Birds such as blue jays, thrushes, robins, and waxwings may be voracious feeders on the ripe fruit from the tree. Ground birds such as pheasant and grouse and rodents such as squirrels, voles, and mice may pick up the food from the ground while even large animals such as deer, cattle, and bears may feed from the tree. The mammal or bird is therefore granted a reward, the pulpy fruit of the hawthorn, for dispersing the hard nutlets inside it, to be passed out at an undetermined time and location. Thus, hawthorn seed is mainly distributed a few meters to a kilometer or so from source. Germination of the nutlets, if they have landed in a favorable spot, may be in the spring after arrival, or in more northern species, often not until the second spring.

CHAPTER *3*

Practical Value

Hawthorns and medlars have a wide variety of uses for humans, although in most cases they are not used as much as certain related genera such as *Malus* (apple) and *Pyrus* (pear). In this chapter we will look at hawthorns and medlars from the viewpoints of food, medicine, ornament, pomology and turnery, agricultural and wildlife values, and erosion control. Ethnobotanical uses generally refer to traditional uses in medicine, for food, or other purposes, and because many of these continue to this day, I do not make a separate section for this subject.

FOR FOOD

The use of hawthorn and medlar fruits for food is probably at least as old as the human race. Casual picking by people has most likely been commonplace wherever superior fruit have not been abundant and may have been important to North American aboriginal people in times of food shortage (Moerman 1998). In North America, traditional Indian cultures have used many hawthorns for food, fresh, dried, or made into cakes, jellies, and so forth (Moerman 1998). I have tasted the ripe fruit of nearly all North American and several Eurasian species. In general, the fruit, although frequently very attractive in appearance, is more disappointing in the mouth. The flesh is mealy to succulent and nearly tasteless to fairly sweet, with various mild fruity odors and tastes that are difficult to pinpoint. In a few cases, however, the taste is very attractive. The fruit contains a good range of vitamins and minerals, though not in large amounts. Values for tejocote (*Crataegus mexicana*) may be considered typical; the amounts listed are per 100 grams edible portion (after CAP-KNAP):

Food energy	8.9 cal.	Calcium	8.2 mg
Moisture	74.8 %	Phosphorus	28 mg
Protein	0.7 gm	Fe (Iron)	18 mg
Fat	0.3 gm	Vitamin A	835 mg
Total CHO	23.5 gm	Thiamine	0.3 mg
(Carbohydrate)		Riboflavin	0.04 mg
Fiber	2.4 gm	Niacin	0.04 mg
Ash	0.7 gm	Ascorbic acid	79 mg
		Refuse	37 mg

Some species have substantial amounts of vitamins A and C. Each fruit, generally 0.5–1 cm in diameter, is full of very hard pyrenes ("seeds") that have to be spat out. In Mexico, and perhaps some other countries in poorer regions, the fruit of wild hawthorns may be methodically collected; however, just a few species have been developed beyond the wild type and show a more general promise for fruit. These are discussed next.

The common medlar (*Mespilus germanica*) has a large fruit, 3–4(–7) cm in diameter in cultivated kinds, though considerably smaller in wild types. Brownish when ripe (Plate 74) and full of large pyrenes, the fruit has to be "bletted" (allowed to partially decay) before the attractive and unusual flavors are released. Prior to bletting, it is harder and sour. Few persons in modern society have tasted medlar, yet it is an experience worth achieving. A specialist company in England markets a medlar jelly (Figure 3.1). 'Nottingham' is a good cultivar for fruit. A fascinating paper by Baird and Thieret (1989) gives many historical references to the gastronomic properties of the medlar and detailed evaluations of the remarkable taste.

The azarole (*Crataegus azarolus*) is a minor fruit of the Mediterranean region. Cultivated forms have a much larger fruit than do most wild hawthorns. The ripe azarole is yellowish or orange and up to 3.5 cm in diameter in cultivated forms. Like all hawthorns, the fruit lacks a crispy texture and has large pyrenes; it reportedly has an applelike flavor. Azarole is a good curiosity for mild climates. Related species like *C. tanacetifolia* and *C. orientalis* are used for the same purpose in Turkey and Armenia, respectively.

The southern United States gives us Mayhaws (any species in series *Aestivales*, for example, *Crataegus aestivalis*, *C. opaca*, and *C. rufula*), so-called because along the Gulf Coast the fruit may ripen as early as May. Mayhaws are used for conserves and pies and are also fermented for wine (Figure 3.2). They are probably one of the best edible fruits in the genus due to a relatively high pectin content and attractive fla-

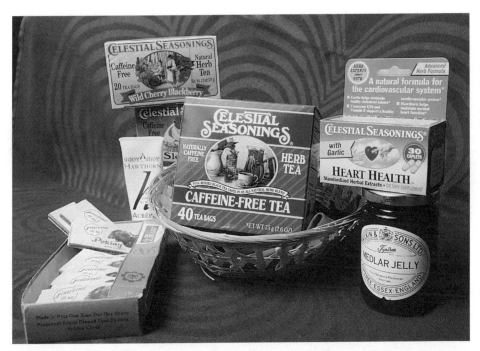

Figure 3.1. Hawthorn and medlar products: herbal teas made with hawthorn fruits and leaves (Celestial Seasonings), hand cream (Body Shop), and wrapped gum-style candy (Peking Candies, China); medlar jam (Wilkin and Sons). (photo A. Noon)

vor. Fruits may be up to 2 cm in diameter and are generally bright red when fully ripe, although some yellow forms are known (Plates 15, 16). Formerly they were only collected from the wild but even so the scale was locally quite large, up to 27,000 kg per year from around Catahoula Lake in Louisiana according to Glen Melcher (pers. comm.). Now an expanding market exists for Mayhaws and they are both propagated and grown commercially on a small scale. Several cultivars are in commerce, and breeding for improved forms takes place. Mayhaws have even reached the attention of the United States Department of Agriculture in Tifton, Georgia, which has a minor crop division.

In southern highland Mexico and some of the Central and South American countries may be found the tejocote (*Crataegus mexicana*), a name actually applied to all Mexican hawthorn species. This species commonly reaches local markets and has also undergone a modest degree of development. I have seen clonal tejocote in

Figure 3.2. Wine, syrup, and preserves made from Mayhaws. (photo G. Melcher)

Puebla State of a superior thornless, large-fruited cultivar with pomes 2.5 cm in diameter (Plate 40). As with other species, the wild type has smaller fruit, and self-sown specimens may show characteristics between wild and fully selected types. Tejocote fruit normally ranges in color between a brilliant chrome yellow and a bright copper-orange (Plates 38, 39). *Crataegus mexicana* is also reported from some Andean parts of Peru and Ecuador where it is known as *C. stipulosa*. Mexicans eat the fruit of many hawthorns, though only *C. mexicana* seems to be specifically cultivated. In gardens and fields in Mexico, large-fruited forms of *C. rosei* subsp. *rosei*, *C. rosei* subsp. *parryana*, *C. gracilior*, *C. greggiana* var. *pepo*, as well as *C. tracyi* var. *madrensis*, may be found. These situations probably represent the beginning of the domestication process where a wild tree is left standing in a field or garden if it has useful fruit. Fruit of wild-type *C. greggiana* are also collected by villagers in dry, poverty-stricken parts of Coahuila State (Plate 7).

In China the species of choice in the north is *Crataegus pinnatifida* in its large-fruited variety *major* (Plate 51). This variety has been substantially cultivated and marketed; up to 50,000 kg of bright red fruits are sold annually. The fruit of *C. pinnatifida* is also fermented for wine on a small scale. A red- to yellow-fruited species, *C. scabrifolia*, superficially resembling *C. mexicana*, occurs in the southwest, in Yunnan, and reaches local markets. In China, hawthorn-flavored candies are marketed (Figure 3.1).

FOR MEDICINE

Hawthorns have a long medicinal history in China and Europe, and a more recent one in North America. Extracts of fruit, leaves, or flowers are used. In China, there is a widespread belief that extracts of hawthorn help digestion and ease diarrhea (Dai and Liu 1982, Pharmacopeia Commission 1992, Bensky and Gamble 1993). Fresh berries of *Crataegus pinnatifida* (sha zhan) are used in the northern part of the country for the first purpose and partially charred fruit for the latter. In southwestern China *C. scabrifolia* is used for the same purposes. Moerman (1998) has collated a number of examples of hawthorn use in North America for bladder trouble, diarrhea, and gynecological matters. In Europe *C. monogyna*, *C. laevigata*, and presumably other related species have a long history of use as an antispasmodic, a sedative, and in the treatment of insomnia and kidney and bladder stones. Some useful general references to medicinal values are as follows: Chevalier (1996), Chiej (1984), Launert (1981), Lawrence Review (1994), Newall et al. (1996), Ody (1993), Reynolds (1989), and Wickham (1981).

The current use for circulatory problems apparently derives from an Irish physician who started using hawthorn extracts in the 19th century. Interestingly, the Cherokee used infusions of *Crataegus spathulata* to ease circulation. There is clear experimental evidence, using anesthetized rabbits, that blood pressure can be lowered and that *Crataegus* extracts are vasodilatory. The active ingredients appear to be certain flavonoids, a large class of compounds famous as plant pigments but clearly with other functions. Some amines and other substances may also be implicated. As with many drugs, over-large doses may be toxic. *Crataegus monogyna* and *C. laevigata* are principally used for hypertension in Europe, but *C. azarolus* and *C. nigra* may also be useful in this context. Many commercial preparations are now available, such as Cratamed®, Crategutt®, Esbericard®, Eurython®, and Oxacant®. Obviously these should not be used without medical advice. The Colorado firm of Celestial Seasonings markets a hawthorn tea, and Body Shop makes a hawthorn hand cream (Figure 3.1).

With 140–200 species of hawthorn, some apparently not closely related to those so far mentioned in this chapter, a large potential exists to be investigated for health purposes.

FOR ORNAMENT

Hawthorns and medlars are widely prized as ornamental shrubs, and almost any species has the potential of creating an average or better horticultural specimen. Billowing clouds of white flowers in spring create the first landscape effect, followed in summer by the neat green foliage and in the autumn by fruit of virtually any color known, except true blues and white, with reds being the most common, then purple, black, and yellow. In spite of this variety, only a few kinds of hawthorn appear regularly in commerce. *Crataegus monogyna* and *C.* ×*media* and cultivars (the latter usually offered as *C. laevigata* or *C. oxyacantha* cultivars), *C. phaenopyrum*, selected forms and cultivars of *C. crus-galli*, and *C. viridis* cultivars are widely offered by nurseries as is the interspecific hybrid *C.* ×*lavallei* (a hardy offspring of *C. mexicana*) and *C.* 'Toba' (offspring of *C. monogyna* × *C. succulenta*).

In the *Crataegus* ×*media* group fine reddish floral colors have been developed, hues hardly routine in wild species. 'Paul's Scarlet' (synonym 'Paulii') is a handsome double rose-red cultivar, and 'Punicea' is a fine single rich red. In North America 'Rubra Plena', with pinkish-mauve flowers, is widely grown, though erroneously as 'Paul's Scarlet'. These are covered in more detail in chapter 7. Most hawthorns and medlars have white flowers, and virtually all of these are attractive and some, spectacular, in flower.

The fruit is perhaps the single most striking ornamental characteristic of hawthorns and medlars, that of virtually any species being attractive if well-grown and not diseased. Its quantity, as attested by some of the photographs in this book, can be immense. A short list would be invidious, though any of the kinds most commonly cultivated would surely rank highly. Reds and reddish oranges predominate; deep reds, purples, and blacks are not rare; a few species have yellow fruit, and others have varieties with yellow fruit. Specimens of *Crataegus* series *Coccineae* that I have seen loaded with fruit are among the finest wild shrubs at that part of their yearly cycle. *Mespilus germanica* has an intriguing brownish fruit, and a white form of *C. brachyacantha* was once noted in Louisiana but never re-found. There are no true blues as in dogwood (*Cornus*), for instance, but the blueberry haw (*Crataegus brachyacantha*) is sometimes "blue" (Plate 18). The truth is that the fruit of *C. brachyacantha* is black when fully ripe, although younger fruit may have purplish tones with an overlay of white waxy bloom (as on grapes), giving the blue-tinted appearance found in blueberries. By the same token, attractive pinks and mauves due to waxy covering are found on the ripe fruits of series *Pruinosae* (frosted thorns).

Hawthorn and medlar fruit varies in size from 4 mm to 2.5 cm in diameter (even larger in some cultivars), in number of fruit per cluster, and in orientation of the cluster (erect, pendulous), each of these variables affecting the total ornamental impact. Some species exhibit a striking and attractive color change during ripening; for instance, the fruit of *Crataegus okanaganensis* is scarlet in late August, changing through purple to finally a dull purple-black at full ripeness, and some forms of *C. chrysocarpa* change from pale yellow through pale orange to deep salmon and finally scarlet at full ripeness.

Autumn color is an important feature and a number of species can have exceptional foliage color. These include *Crataegus brachyacantha*, *C. chrysocarpa* var. *piperi*, some genotypes of *C. crus-galli*, *C. fecunda*, *C. macracantha* var. *occidentalis*, *C. okanaganensis*, *C. phaenopyrum*, most members of series *Pruinosae* and series *Purpureofructi*, members of series *Intricatae* and series *Pulcherrimae*, the hybrid *C.* ×*persimilis*, and so forth. The common medlar is no dullard either, its foliage "one mass of nankeen and crimson" (Coleman 1885) and "endless contrasts of green, yellow, orange, russet, and red . . . (nearly all . . . indeed) may be found on one leaf" (Boulger 1907).

Plant habit should not be ignored as an ornamental characteristic. Trees 9 m tall can easily be had with the right genotypes of *Crataegus brachyacantha*, *C. coccinea*, *C. crus-galli*, *C. holmesiana*, *C. mollis*, *C. monogyna*, *C. okennonii*, *C. phaenopyrum*, and *C. viridis*. Many species are smaller than this and take on an attractive, gnarled appearance when older while others can make interesting thickets of suckering shrubs. Most forms of *C. punctata* and several forms of *C. crus-galli* have well-defined layered branching which is very attractive. Possibly the finest ornamental medlar or hawthorn is Stern's medlar, *Mespilus canescens*, which is a veritable fountain of thornless shoots, gray-green leaves, very large flowers, pretty bright scarlet fruit, and tight clusters of slender trunks arching upwards and outwards, not unlike *Kolkwitzia* (Plate 73). This species also has attractive flaking bark.

Bark should not be neglected as an ornamental asset. The bark of most species of hawthorn (for example, *Crataegus gattingeri*) is fibrous shredding with orange tones on the newly exposed surfaces (Plate 8), but a few, such as *C. spathulata* (Plate 9) and forms of *C. viridis*, have instead an attractive, smooth, scaling bark. *Crataegus spathulata* is worth growing for this trait alone. A small number of hawthorns possess smooth bark with horizontal lenticels, ornamentally like superior *Prunus maackii*; one such example is *C. saligna* (Figure 7.10).

The Achilles' heels of some hawthorns, which in certain seasons can be quite serious ornamentally, include attacks of rust or tent caterpillar, defoliation due to drought, damage to or loss of the fruit crop by disease or drought, early fall of fruit, and suckering. A species like *Crataegus phaenopyrum*, the Washington thorn, has many of the better qualities, its white flowers, glossy green foliage, attractive autumnal foliage color, and brilliant orange-red fruit with smart black "eye" resisting well many kinds of disease and pest. Adequate irrigation during dry periods helps to ensure good fruit and foliage. The length of time that fruit hangs on the bush is an important horticultural consideration. Unfortunately, it is often not long except in selected kinds or species; however, almost any hawthorn that can be grown well (free of disease, well-watered, and with no midsummer defoliation due to heat) should be attractive in fruit, flower, and leaf while a number possess interesting habit or beautiful bark.

FOR POMOLOGY AND TURNERY

Hawthorns are graft-compatible with pears (*Pyrus*) and a certain amount of experimentation to obtain a dwarfing stock hardier than quince (*Cydonia*) has been attempted. Unfortunately, the thorny, suckering nature of the understock has not led to significant progress in this direction. As pointed out earlier, however, there is perhaps serious potential in the development of less thorny *Crataegus* understock. It is also reported that *C. pinnatifida* is used as an understock for apples in Shandong Province, China.

Hawthorn wood is extremely hard due to the slow growth of the trunk and it has been greatly prized for turnery for which the azarole has been used in Europe (Christensen 1992). At most, however, insignificant quantities enter commerce. Montana Indians made digging tools, pins, and fishhooks from the very hard wood of hawthorn (Moerman 1998). It should be remembered in this context that the Latin generic name *Crataegus* is derived from the Greek *kratos*, meaning "hard."

For Agricultural Husbandry
and Wildlife Values

The thorny and shrubby nature of hawthorns has made them good hedging plants. In fact, the word *haw*, now used for the fruit alone, meant "hedge" in Anglo-Saxon. Many hawthorn species are excellent choices for a hedge, even a stock-proof hedge. Hawthorns are dense, thorny, and often branched to the ground, and their branches are hard and tough, relatively resistant to the shoving of heavy domestic animals. Hawthorns are still widely used for hedges, both for practical purposes, usually agricultural, and for ornamental use.

Crataegus monogyna has been the most widely planted species for hedges, but a considerable number of hawthorn species could make excellent hedges—experimentation is in order. In Russia the ultra-hardy *C. sanguinea* has been used (Pojarkova 1939). The value of *C. monogyna* as a hedge lies in its ability to thrive under regular and intense trimming or browsing, and in the density of branches of the resulting hedge. Ornamentally, the numerous glossy, deep green leaves make a *C. monogyna* hedge opaque during the growing season and leaf loss in the fall reveals a fine tracery of branchlets. Only a few flowers and fruit can be expected in regularly trimmed hedges. Of the native shrubs available in Europe, *C. monogyna* is one of the very best for hedges and it is still commercially produced in large quantity for this purpose.

Hedges today are also often used horticulturally either for privacy around a property, or decoratively, but for these purposes a huge array of different shrubs, trees, and subshrubs may be utilized. One of the most remarkable hedges in history was the Great Hedge of India (Moxham 2000), a 1280-kilometer section of the 3680-kilometer customs barrier of mid-19th-century India, established to enforce the salt tax. A workforce of 10,000 to 14,000 was required for enforcement and to maintain the barrier; however, being tropical, this hedge was not of hawthorn.

In the countryside, hedges are one means of demarcating property or subdividing it into individual fields. In rocky regions stone walls have been traditionally built. In modern times, especially in large open areas, fences of either barbed wire or a smooth electrified wire are used. In some regions linear banks of earth, or alternatively ditches, divide land. Another method of enclosing land is by the wooden fence and this also has a long history in agricultural Europe. Oliver Rackham (1994) draws attention to two main types of lowland agricultural landscape in Europe: open-field and hedged (Plate 10). These seem to be traditional and have in

many cases co-existed in the same area for centuries. Because of the cultural significance of hawthorn hedges, particularly of *Crataegus monogyna*, I develop here an
analysis of agricultural value of hedges.

Agricultural hedges have been generated in three main ways: by planting, by
natural invasion along a fence line (usually a wire fence in modern times), or, in the
case of ancient hedges in Europe, by being left behind in the early days of woodland
clearance, sometimes well over 1000 years ago. In the early settlement of lowland
England when the Saxons moved on to the clay soils which they could cultivate
with their plough, fields were cleared and strips of brush and woodland left between
them, incipient hedges. Some existing hedges, those with greatest floral diversity,
date back to this time. Perhaps we could learn from the past in this context?

Hawthorns are more amenable to maintenance than many other woody species
because they grow back well from severe pruning. As a result the traditional British way to maintain a hedge was to regularly "plash" or "lay" it (often wrongly
written "layering"). This method involved allowing upright trunks to develop to
3.6–6 m tall and 5–7.5 cm in diameter, then partially severing them low down
with a diagonal slash from a billhook, and "laying" the detached trunk at a flat
diagonal along the hedge line. These pieces would be secured with uprights left
standing and then the whole trimmed to a height of 1.5–1.8 m, as shown in Plate
11. In this example, however, the uprights are stakes driven into the ground. The
process requires renewal every 10–20 years. Hawthorn hedges, to be effective enclo-
sures for livestock, require regular maintenance by agricultural laborers who do
this work in winter. The task is not highly paid but quite highly skilled. In modern times, hedges are often maintained by mechanical trimming (Plate 12), and
while this may facilitate maintenance it does nothing to maintain the structure of
the hedge and gaps will gradually develop which require attention.

Agricultural hedges have various pros and cons as discussed in detail in the
excellent book *Hedges* (Pollard et al. 1974). Some of the advantages are as follows.
First, hedges act as a windbreak and the resultant reduction of evapotranspiration
is generally beneficial to the crop. This benefit will generally more than cancel out
the effect of the land taken up for the hedge together with the adjacent narrow area
where there is root competition with the crop (see Figure 3.3). Without doubt,
hedges retard both wind and water erosion by intercepting runoff. This fact is so
evident that in some countries (for example, Hungary) extensive shelter belts have
been planted up to 15 m wide and many kilometers long. Count all these hedges
as environmentally friendly for they also provide a rich habitat for a great variety of
wildflowers if not subject to too intense spray drift from agricultural chemicals.

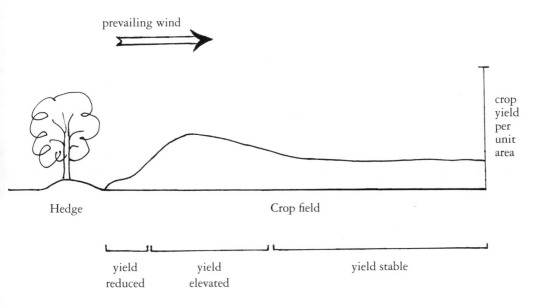

prevailing wind

crop
yield
per
unit
area

Hedge   Crop field

yield   yield   yield stable
reduced   elevated

Figure 3.3. Schematic showing effect of hedge competition and wind protection on crop yields. Values will vary according to actual evapotranspiration values under differing soil, crop, and weather regimes.

Hedgerows are a fine habitat, too, for smaller forms of wildlife, although the population of pestilential rodents such as voles and mice therein has to be taken into account objectively and on the basis of local experience. Contrariwise, a good supply of birds of prey, foxes, and snakes, which also like the hedgerow habitat, provide a countervailing force. In addition, hedges with some shelter trees, or simply shelter belts, can be important for sheltering stock from intense summer heat or severe hail and this may save on veterinary costs. The growth of trees in hedges for timber purposes has often been considered as a major economic asset to a farm in traditional European husbandry. In all cases, of course, hedgerow management needs to be skillful to maintain the desired result.

We now turn to the negative side of the case for hedges. First, they fossilize the field arrangement and do not permit flexibility in changing field boundaries. Today fields often need to be larger than in previous times to handle modern machinery. Certainly there is nothing so inexpensive and flexible as the single wire electrified fence attached to thin (1.25 cm in diameter) steel posts that characterizes Swiss agriculture. Second, hedges may appear to be costly to create and maintain. Third, hedges take up space. Figure 3.4 shows the loss of productive ground as a percent of the whole with fields of 5, 10, 20, 50, and 200 hectares. In larger fields, however, one can see that these losses are simply insignificant. My calculations are for square fields. The narrower or more irregular the shape of a field, the greater the fraction of edge. Finally, it is sometimes felt that hedge lines are a source of pests and disease. The issue of hedges as a weed source is generally easily dealt with. The hedge habitat is so different from that of the cultivated field that it is not a significant source of agricultural weed seeds. Pathogens, on the other hand, may sometimes represent a more serious issue, and one cannot recommend hawthorn hedges around apple orchards in North America anymore than blackthorn (*Prunus spinosa*) hedges

Figure 3.4. Relationship between square field total area and area of land devoted to partition (hedges, grass strips, fences, and so forth).

Let l = length of side
Let w = width of partition
Then w ÷ 2 = width of partition applicable to one of the fields, and
$2wl-w^2$ = total area taken up by partition in one field
Note: 1 hectare = 10,000 sq m

RELATIONSHIP BETWEEN FIELD AREA AND LENGTH OF SIDE

Field size (ha)	5	10	20	50	200
Length of side (m)	224	316	447	707	1,414

TOTAL AREA OF HEDGE ALLOWANCE (SQ M)

No partition	0	0	0	0	0
Partition 1 m wide	447	631	893	1,413	2,827
Partition 2 m wide	892	1,260	1,784	2,824	5,652
Partition 5 m wide	2,215	3,135	4,445	7,045	14,115

FIELD AREA DEVOTED TO PARTITION (%)

At 0 m wide	0.00	0.00	0.00	0.00	0.00
At 1 m wide	0.89	0.63	0.45	0.28	0.14
At 2 m wide	1.78	1.26	0.89	0.56	0.28
At 5 m wide	4.43	3.14	2.22	1.41	0.71

around plum orchards in Europe unless these are sprayed for pests and disease too. Before the invention of wire as an alternative, most of the arguments against hedges were meaningless, however, today they have to be evaluated.

Whereas many hedges have disappeared to make fields large enough for modern agriculture it would seem that many of those remaining could be allowed to continue with benefit. In England legal steps have recently been taken to reduce the extinction of hedges (Wolton 1999). In Europe, the invasion of hawthorn hedges by blackberries or brambles (*Rubus fruticosus* agg.) and hazel (*Corylus avellana*) provides a late summer and fall bounty for local people, while wild roses (*Rosa*) provide color and hips rich in vitamin C. Hedgerows are a major scenic element in much of lowland northwestern Europe, parts of Italy, Poland, Russia, Crete, and Spain and fill an aesthetic role in the traditional landscape (Plate 10). In England, parts of Normandy, and the Ardennes in Belgium, hawthorn hedges may still be seen aplenty although their total length is diminishing. That they were perfectly well known to the Romans also is clear from the writer Colonella. In many parts of North America natural hedges now occur along old fence lines though few are deliberately planted in this continent. In eastern Ontario, large natural hedges of hawthorns, particularly *Crataegus submollis*, are quite common along fence lines. Similarly, in the northern Okanagan of British Columbia beautiful and fascinating multispecies natural hedges mainly of hawthorn manifest a variety of fruit and leaf colors in late summer and early autumn. In North America, however, these rural hedge lines are not managed.

FOR EROSION CONTROL

Landscaping on a large scale can use hawthorns to create thickets and develop an effective answer to erosion. In spite of this potential, most examples of thickets that one encounters are natural, rather than human-engineered. A large field of perhaps 400 hectares on a hillside in Grey County, Ontario, is one of the finest such examples that I have encountered. In this case a sloping field was originally ploughed, began to develop sheet and gully erosion, and was then abandoned for cultivation. Some 20 years later, it has become largely a hawthorn thicket, with intermittent cattle gazing. It is unrealistic to return this to the plough, but the erosion has been stopped, soil-forming processes are being renewed, and the landowner now has a choice between succession to deciduous forest or maintaining a somewhat *Crataegus*-invaded pasture.

Nuisance Aspects of Hawthorns

Hawthorns are often strong competitors in pastures in mesic areas or on mesic sites in drier areas and are often looked upon with disfavor by farmers who may therefore wish to eradicate or control them. Numerous landowners have described to us tires ruined from running over hawthorns, which adds to the dislike felt by many farmers. Eradication or control is also sometimes sought near apple orchards where hawthorns are one of the alternate hosts for cedar-apple rust, sometimes a serious pathogen of apples. In Nova Scotia the provincial government, as long ago as 1933, passed an act to control the apple maggot (*Rhagoletis pomonella*) which involved, in part, attempts to eradicate all hawthorns (another host for *Rhagoletis*) in the apple growing regions of the province. This act was still being implemented as late as 1999. Nevertheless, widespread control or eradication specifically of hawthorns is not often practiced except as part of the indiscriminate destruction of all scrubby vegetation that often accompanies farming.

CHAPTER *4*

Cultivation

M OST HAWTHORNS and medlars are easy to cultivate if provided basic soil and climatic requirements. Some, however, are easier and more pest-free than others, a factor to be considered when choosing what kinds to grow in an ornamental garden. This chapter deals with hardiness, soils, planting, pruning, propagation, and pests and diseases.

HARDINESS

Hawthorn species occur in much of the north temperate zone. The southernmost species are found in the subtropical parts of southern China, the mild temperate parts of the southern Mexican and Guatemalan highlands, around the U.S. Gulf Coast, and around the Mediterranean. All these areas include regions where temperatures as low as −5°C are rare and where the growing season is long and fairly hot. Northwards, certain species reach the Hudson Bay lowlands in Canada, the mountains of northern Kazakhstan in central Asia, and the parts of Siberia to the north of Mongolia and China. All these regions have much colder winters than the main temperate area of distribution, with coldest temperatures down to at least −40°C, and have a much shorter growing season. The range of hardiness zones involved for all species, using the U.S. standard, is from 8 or 9 (mildest) to 2 (harshest). In the great west-east temperature cline of winter Europe this equates to Atlantic coastal (zones 8 or 9) to well east of Moscow (zone 2).

Species occupying the different parts of such a wide climatic range cannot be expected to perform equally well everywhere. Our experience in North America is

that Gulf Coast and Mexican species rarely survive in the southern Great Lakes–
southern New England area (zones 5–6). Nevertheless, in most temperate parts of
the world within hardiness zones 4–7 one may expect to be able to cultivate a wide
range of hawthorns, but there is no single location known to me where they can all
be expected to perform well. Expected winter survivability is commonly up to two
climatic zones colder than that of the native habitat. A species like *Crataegus mexicana*, which might be expected to survive routinely in parts of the Mediterranean
area, was repeatedly introduced to southern England and northern France in the
19th century but failed to survive their coldest winters. There is also hardiness
variation within individual species that possess a large geographical range, plants
from more northern provenances (more eastern in most of Europe) having the
potential of being hardier than others of the same species from further south. Therefore, because many *Crataegus* species have not been extensively cultivated, knowledge of provenance has to substitute for hardiness zones. This book indicates the
natural geographical ranges of the species and also includes winter-hardiness maps
for North America, Europe, and East Asia to enable readers to reach their own deci-
sions on the probable hardiness of most species. The zone numbers for all three
maps are based on the United States Department of Agriculture's numerical rating
system: the higher the number the warmer the zone. The average annual minimum temperature ranges are as follows:

CELSIUS	ZONE	FAHRENHEIT
Below −46	Zone 1	Below −50
−46 to −40	Zone 2	−50 to −40
−40 to −35	Zone 3	−40 to −30
−35 to −29	Zone 4	−30 to −20
−29 to −23	Zone 5	−20 to −10
−23 to −18	Zone 6	−10 to 0
−18 to −12	Zone 7	0 to 10
−12 to −7	Zone 8	10 to 20
−7 to −1	Zone 9	20 to 30
−1 to 4	Zone 10	30 to 40
5 and Above	Zone 11	40 and Above

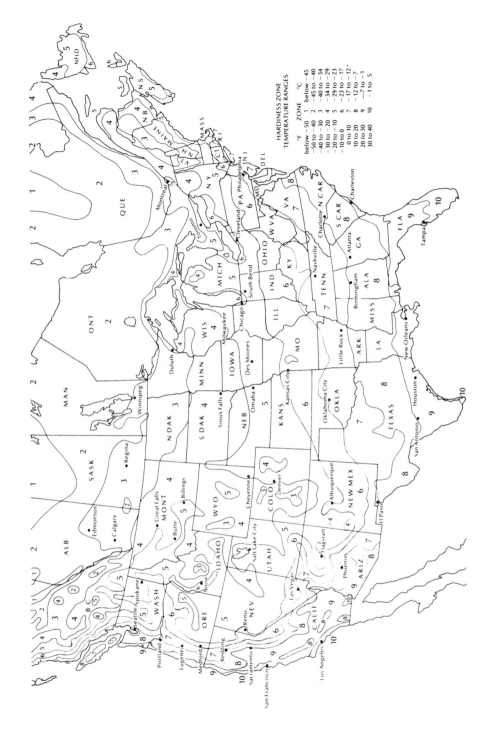

Figure 4.1. Hardiness zones of North America based on USDA hardiness zones.

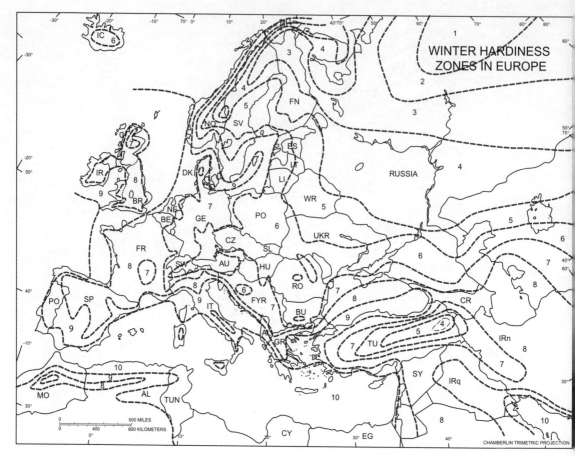

Figure 4.2. Hardiness zones of Europe and western Asia based on USDA hardiness zones.
J. B. Phipps, after Heinze and Schreibe (1984).

SOILS

Most hawthorns flourish on clay-loam soils and many, especially from drier areas,
appear to be distinct calciphiles. Many species are quite tolerant of wet feet and all
species of series *Aestivales* normally grow in such habitats. In contrast, species of the
southeastern United States series *Lacrimatae* flourish in a sharply drained soil and are
markedly xeromorphic in nature. Nearly all species, however, are easily cultivated
in good, well-drained garden soil with supplemental water in dry periods.

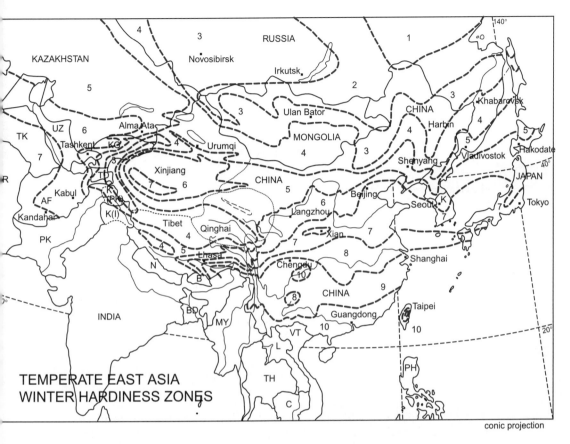

Figure 4.3. Hardiness zones of temperate East Asia based on USDA hardiness zones. Compiled by M. Widrlechner, U.S. Department of Agriculture, University of Iowa. Used with permission.

PLANTING AND SUBSEQUENT CARE

The requirements for successful planting are identical to those for most other deciduous woody plants. Transplanting is most successful when the plant is leafless, between late fall and early spring but not in subzero (Celsius) temperatures. Moving the plant with a good root-ball, well tied up ("balled and burlapped") is best, though smaller plants may move well bare-root so long as the exposed roots are not allowed to desiccate or freeze in the process. Staking is advisable in windy locations until new roots are established and reasonably generous watering during dry periods in the first two summers is important to survival. Although many hawthorns are somewhat xeromorphic, irrigation in dry summers is important to prevent defoliation and help fruit retention. Modest fertilization with slow-acting low-nitrogen general fertilizer is helpful when plants are young.

PRUNING

Hawthorns are best pruned dormant in late winter to early spring before bud-burst. With larger kinds, it may be desirable to prune to a good leader. Sharp tools should be used. Also suckering is serious with some understocks and with some species. With grafted kinds it is important not to allow any suckers a chance to establish, or they could take over the scion. If a tree is grown on its own roots suckering might be permitted but one would then develop a small thicket of the hawthorn in question. There is generally not much point in thinning the upper part of a hawthorn bush or small tree since the natural growth form is dense.

PROPAGATION

Hawthorns may be propagated by seed, by cuttings, and by grafting. Seed is a generally reliable method though there may be problems due to infertility and lack of true breeding in desirable hybrids including some of the best cultivars. Cuttings are generally very hard to root and require specialist knowledge while grafting is the preferred commercial technique for reproduction. These matters will be discussed further below.

The seeds of hawthorns and medlars are tiny flakes of tissue embedded in the hard bony pyrenes in the center of each haw. They are quite difficult to extract from the pyrenes and the latter are usually planted whole as if individual seeds. Germination of northern hawthorns (native to zone 7 or lower) usually requires stratification for two winters while more southern hawthorns (zone 8 or higher) usually germinate after one winter. Double winter dormancy may be broken by treating the dry pyrenes with concentrated sulfuric acid for up to 4 hours (Young and Young 1992). It should be noted that the times for acid scarification vary between species and also that most horticultural authors speaking of hawthorn "seed" mean the pyrene or nutlet. Pyrenes are best planted in a shallow pan or flat covered with a thin mesh to prevent disturbance and left at ambient temperatures. After germination the young seedlings may be allowed to grow their first two or three leaves, and then they should be carefully pricked out into larger pots. Subsequent care is similar to that for other woody plants.

Cuttings are generally reckoned in the horticultural literature to be virtually impossible to root, but an English firm (Gosler et al. 1994) has had considerable success with *Crataegus monogyna* cuttings. Also, several nurseries in Louisiana routinely propagate *C. opaca* cultivars by cuttings. It is clear that more general experimentation with this very important method of propagation is necessary. Apparently, the use of extremely young, still growing, greenwood cuttings treated with rooting hormone represents the best method of rooting Mayhaws (Craft et al. 1996). The very tender growing tips of these should be removed. Such cuttings need to be kept under mist and also be sheltered from direct sunlight until well rooted. Subsequent care would be routine for shrubs grown from cuttings. Also, hardwood cuttings of Mayhaws, collected in fall and allowed to callus at their lower end while waxed at the upper end, may root in the spring.

Commercially desirable strains of hawthorn or medlar are usually propagated by grafting onto *Crataegus* rootstock. Almost any hawthorn species is probably compatible, but *C. monogyna* and *C. phaenopyrum* are commonly used. Grafting is a simple and effective method of cloning where cuttings cannot be made to take. Grow sufficient understock from seed and graft dormant scions in spring about bud-burst or bud them in fairly late summer. If conducted in the open, both operations are best carried out in overcast and mild weather. Otherwise budding is done onto actively growing stocks in a lath house or grafting onto dormant stocks (bench-grafting) in the winter at 2–5°C.

PESTS AND DISEASES

In North America, hawthorns are susceptible to a variety of troublesome pests and diseases. The most serious is cedar-hawthorn rust (caused by *Gymnosporangium*), a disfiguring disease of red cedar (*Juniperus virginiana*) and most, if not all, species of *Crataegus*. The causative agent is a fungus which passes different parts of its life-cycle on red cedar and hawthorn and requires both hosts to survive. Removing all the juniper in the neighborhood may help the hawthorns, but this is a task that could either be illegal or prohibitively expensive or require the co-operation of many landowners. Moreover, the very light spores of *Gymnosporangium* are carried many kilometers in the wind so clearing a relatively small area would confer only limited protection. Spraying very young leaves with a systemic fungicide, such as benomyl, effects a temporary cure but has to be done each season. In some areas rust is so prevalent that the ornamental value of susceptible hawthorns is greatly reduced. Nevertheless, some species (for example, *C. phaenopyrum*) appear to be quite resistant to the rust. The pictures in this book have been primarily selected to illustrate healthy hawthorns, but some rust can be seen on the foliage of *Crataegus* sp. aff. *C. chrysocarpa* (Plate 13, leaf near top right).

Fireblight (*Erwinia*) of apples, a bacterial disease, may also affect hawthorns, although the North American species of *Crataegus* show a good deal of resistance. The antibiotic streptomycin, in a commercial formulation such as Agristrep®, effects some control; however, in the author's experience, fireblight is not a particularly serious disease of hawthorn.

In North America, a species of tent caterpillar, *Malacosoma americana*, preferentially attacks rosaceous woody plants. Although severe infestation is episodic, total defoliation can sometimes result and bad attacks in successive years may result in death of the plant. Control may be had by dormant spray (the adult moth lays egg masses that surround the twig) or other insecticide on the young larvae in which case a surfactant is probably necessary to penetrate the web. In the home garden where only few hawthorns are grown, it is easy enough and more environmentally friendly to remove the young larvae by hand as soon as the webs appear by rubbing a piece of tautly held twine or small bundle of grass stems around the branch joints where they congregate.

Another quite common problem, which disfigures foliage and presumably significantly weakens the plant when there is a severe infestation, is a gall-like growth along the leaves, often close to the veins, that resembles the coxcomb aphid gall of elm (*Colopha ulmicola*). In fairly casual observation it is especially common on *Crataegus williamsii* and *C. macracantha* in the Flathead drainage of Montana. This problem also occurs on other species of hawthorn (see Plates 58, 59).

At Glastonbury, mistletoe (*Viscum album*) was seen growing on *Crataegus monogyna* 'Biflora', but it is not known how common this is. Hawthorns and medlars may, from time to time, suffer from other pests and diseases, but these are not usually of a kind to cause one to think twice about cultivating these plants. Appropriate insecticides and fungicides may be used as needed.

PLANT SOURCES

Most nurseries offer for sale only one to a very few kinds of hawthorn, and in many areas, no medlars. Therefore, such works as *The Anderson Horticultural Library's Source List of Plants and Seeds*, produced by the Minnesota Landscape Arboretum, or *The Plant Finder*, produced by the Royal Horticultural Society, are invaluable for locating commercial sources in North America (the former) or the British Isles (the latter). Other countries may produce similar indices. Arboreta may be a good source of seed and, if you are known to their staff, might supply scionwood for grafting. If, however, you are prepared for the somewhat slow process of growing hawthorns from seed, then natural areas can, in many regions, provide an almost inexhaustible supply of new kinds, generating great interest for the intrepid searcher and introducing you to a new world of beauty and knowledge.

CHAPTER 5

Breeding and Selection

THE POTENTIAL for improving hawthorns for various purposes is enormous. While many species of hawthorn and medlar occur occasionally in commerce, very few do so regularly. This points to the fact that there are clear defects in many wild species as cultivated plants. At the same time, several species have broken these barriers. While several interspecific crosses have been deliberately made, resulting in such interesting hybrids as *Crataegus ×grignonensis*, *C. ×lavallei*, and *C. ×mordenensis*, there has been little systematic effort to improve desirable qualities in the West except for limited efforts by minor fruit breeders particularly with Mayhaws. Some of the better ornamental forms are merely selections from the wild rather than arising from purposeful breeding. Selection from the wild is in any case the fundamental source of new variation. In this chapter we address some of the specific areas of concern.

OBJECTIVES

The primary areas of interest for improvement are the edible quality of the fruit and several ornamental characteristics, particularly those of habit, thorniness, drought resistance, fruit retention, and freedom from disease.

FRUIT FOR CONSUMPTION. The use of hawthorns for fruit was discussed in chapter 3 and, with the exception of Mayhaws, seems to be in decline for several reasons: (1) the large central block of hard pyrenes that have to be spat out if the fruit is fresh, and therefore the proportion of the whole fruit that is edible; (2) poor keeping qualities that require the fruit to be processed or eaten very soon after harvest;

(3) the small size and irregular, but usually early, fall of fruit; (4) the lack of sufficiently distinctive taste characteristics; and (5) the potential of fruit for being badly rusted or otherwise deformed. Of these, the fundamental nature of taste and texture of hawthorn fruit is hardest to address. Genotypes with greatly reduced pyrenes exist in *Crataegus pinnatifida*, and delayed ripening genes exist in several species, for instance, Grey County (Ontario) *C. ? suborbiculata*, and also some other species. Large size is found in genotypes of all species cultivated for fruit but also in some species not cultivated for edible fruit, such as *C. coccinea* and the turkey haw, *C. induta*. Obviously, in the wealth of wild forms there are also bound to be genotypes offering better resistance to pathogens and early dropping of fruit due to drought. It is also possible to mitigate these last two problems by good cultural practice. Thus, there is within *Crataegus* the genetic potential to greatly improve many of the qualities needed in a pomological crop.

FLOWER AND FRUIT COLOR. As far as ornamental horticulture is concerned, the fruit is again of great significance and the enormous range of wild forms provides breeders with a great spectrum of color, varied resistance to pests and bad weather, delayed abscission, and so on. Also, breeding for pink and red, specifically crimson, flower color probably holds promise. All normal hawthorns have white flowers so the source of the reds and pinks in cultivars of *Crataegus monogyna* and *C. ×media* is of interest. I have noted that in many individuals of some hawthorn species the petals turn pink at late anthesis. Also, occasional flowers on mainly white individuals may be bright pink throughout or marked with crimson (Plate 14). It is possible that some of these variants represent a morphogenetic change caused by low temperature damage. If genes controlling these biochemical changes could be located and utilized, then a whole new canvas would be available.

FOLIAGE QUALITY. The question of poor foliage due to pests and dry weather also needs consideration and, again, selection of superior wild forms with an eye to breeding from them, together with good cultural practice, may be the main route to go. Casual observation of hawthorn populations clearly indicates large differences in degree of rust infection between individuals of a single species, but whether this has a genetic basis is not known. An extensive search for rust-resistant hawthorn strains needs implementing. Since hawthorns are very common in many areas, it would be worthwhile searching for wild specimens showing improved resistance to rust and propagating these. Late summer to early fall is a good time to do this because the condition of the leaves (infected/non-infected) will be evident and seed can be collected at the same time.

GROWTH HABIT AND THORNINESS. Two potential problems with the growth habit of the plant may need attention—suckering and thorns. Suckering is certainly a nuisance and selection of weakly suckering genotypes is an obvious breeding aim. Then other kinds could be grafted onto such weakly or non-suckering rootstocks. It should not be difficult to find a range of such form suitable for all climatic areas. Thorniness is less of a problem because fruit is rarely picked by hand, which in any case may be commercially unviable. Thorniness may constitute a problem perhaps for neophyte pruners, though in 25 years of working intensively with hawthorns, I have hardly ever been more than trivially scratched. My worst experience was to step on a branched thorn lying hidden in grass below the canopy of a hawthorn grove while I was wearing lightweight running shoes. This is not an experience to be desired and would not occur among thornless hawthorns or had I been wearing more strongly soled shoes. There is a gene for thornlessness in *Crataegus crus-galli* and a number of species of hawthorn have generally few thorns at maturity, notably *C. scabrifolia*, *C. hupehensis*, *C. mollis*, and *C. calpodendron*. As noted elsewhere, I have encountered a thornless clone of cultivated *C. mexicana* in Puebla State, Mexico.

SIGNIFICANCE OF THE BREEDING SYSTEM

Although all hawthorns are pollinated in the same manner (see chapter 2), they have different strategies for reproductive biology. First, the species may be sexual, in which case pollen is required to carry one set of genes for the next generation. Sexual plants may be self-incompatible (self-sterile) in which case pollen of a different genotype is required to effect fertilization. This situation exists with apples, for instance, where 'MacIntosh' can't fertilize itself. A fair number of diploid hawthorns, generally 20-stamen species, are self-incompatible. *Crataegus viridis* 'Winter King' seems to be such an example, which when there is no other nearby hawthorn flowering at the same time, fails to set fruit. Tetraploids, by contrast, are likely to be self-compatible, as Dickinson et al. (1996) have shown in *C. douglasii*. Finally, many hawthorns are apomictic, need pollination (hence are "pseudogamous") but produce seed only from unreduced female embryo precursors.

The technical approaches to hawthorn breeding are the same as those for most other plants, with one proviso, which is that all triploid hawthorns are apomictic and cannot be readily bred unless they are first rendered hexaploid. Generally speaking one cannot, in fact, breed any apomicts. Many tetraploid forms seem to have a degree of apomixis, but in these cases it is usually, perhaps always, facultative. The existence of polyploidy in hawthorns also necessitates separate breeding programs at each ploidy level unless it were acceptable to generate apomictic triploids. The problem with a promising apomictic triploid is, of course, that it is at the end of the road for breeding purposes without hexaploidization. Before a breeding program can be established therefore, it is necessary to discover both the breeding system and chromosome numbers of one's hawthorns (see also chapter 2).

Chromosomes of *Crataegus* and *Mespilus* are in multiples of 17 (x = 17) which is also true for other members of subfamily Maloideae (apple subfamily) of Rosaceae. Diploids (2x) therefore have 34 chromosomes, triploids (3x) 51 chromosomes, and tetraploids (4x) 68 chromosomes. Chromosome counts can be made by standard techniques of cytology by properly trained individuals, but flow cytometry is recommended for large-scale screening. We have had some success in obtaining chromosome counts using young vegetative buds.

Apomixis is genetically controlled and it could be valuable to breed a highly desirable morphotype that is apomictic, as such a plant would then reproduce true from seed. Apomixis is perhaps best proven cytologically by examining young ovules microscopically for the development of sexual or aposporous (or rarely diplosporous) embryo sacs. Apomixis can, in principle, also be tested for by controlled emasculation followed by checking for seed development in the absence of pollen. This kind of test is complicated by the frequent existence of pseudogamy— the situation where pollination is needed to trigger ovule development even in apomicts. Alternatively, apomixis may be demonstrated by proving genetically maternal offspring. Highly professional levels of technique are necessary to deal with apomixis effectively and knowledgeably.

TECHNIQUES

The actual mechanics of breeding involve controlled pollination in which the flower used to produce seed (female parent) is carefully emasculated when young, pollinated using a fine paint brush with pollen from a known parent, bagged with fine muslin to keep out external pollen sources, and tagged. Careful records are kept of the parents used. The reader may obtain further ideas of methodology and potential from Mayhaws (Craft et al. 1996). There is great potential for expanding the horticultural and pomological uses of hawthorns and medlars by breeding.

PART TWO

The Cast
of Characters

CHAPTER *6*

Classification and Identification

M EDLARS (*Mespilus*) and hawthorns (*Crataegus*) both belong to the rose family (Rosaceae) in the maloid subfamily (Maloideae). The rose family is a large and important, mainly temperate family that generates most of our important temperate fruits: apples, pears, quinces, loquats, service-berries (saskatoons), plums, peaches, apricots, cherries, raspberries, blackberries, and strawberries. It is also important in ornamental horticulture for the small trees in apple, pear, mountain ash, whitebeam, service-tree, peach, and cherry; for the bushes in hawthorn, *Chaenomeles*, *Cotoneaster*, *Heteromeles*, *Neillia*, *Photinia*, *Pyracantha* (firethorn), *Rhaphiolepis*, and *Spiraea*; and for the herbaceous plants in *Alchemilla*, *Aruncus*, *Filipendula*, *Gillenia*, and *Potentilla*, among many others.

The rose family is divided into four subfamilies. Maloideae, one of three woody (small trees or bushes) subfamilies, is the only one with berrylike fruit. Unlike true berries, however, the carpels of Maloideae are uniquely invested by a hypanthium, which thus becomes the outer and fleshy part of the maloid fruit (Plate 6). The fruit of subfamily Amygdaloideae (cherries, plums) are drupes, and the fruit of Spiraeoideae are dry. The remaining subfamily Rosoideae, by far the largest in the rose family, is mostly herbaceous and nearly always has dry fruit. The subfamilies tend to have characteristic base chromosome numbers too, Maloideae being $x = 17$.

Medlars and hawthorns constitute a closely related pair within subfamily Maloideae. They are part of a tribe called Crataegeae wherein the carpellary walls become bony in fruit, generating hard nutlets inside the fleshy hypanthial wall. Other maloid genera with hard nutlets are *Cotoneaster*, *Hesperomeles*, *Osteomeles*, and *Pyracantha*, but each of these is quite different from *Mespilus* and *Crataegus*.

57

CLASSIFICATION. Medlars and hawthorns are not very different from one another and no single character suffices to separate them. The problem became especially difficult consequent on the discovery of *Mespilus canescens* (Phipps 1990), which is rather different from *M. germanica*, and with the recent fuller understanding of *Crataegus triflora*. Some differences are listed here:

CHARACTERISTIC	MEDLAR	HAWTHORN
Plant habit	Usually multitrunked	Usually single-trunk dominance
Leaves	Narrow, nearly entire, camptodromous venation	Broader, usually lobed, usually craspedodromous venation
Flowers	Large, 20–40 stamens, notched petals	Small to large, usually 10 or 20 stamens, petals not notched
Fruit	Containing stone cells, calyx erect	Usually lacking stone cells, calyx usually spreading to reflexed

What is nevertheless clear is that neither medlar is particularly close to any hawthorn species.

Mespilus germanica is native to Balkan Europe, Turkey, Caucasus, and northern Iran. *Mespilus canescens* is native to Arkansas in the United States. The great geographical separation implies long temporal separation, which is reflected in the considerable differences between the two species, the former with its large brown fruit and the latter with its smaller, scarlet, more hawthorn-like fruit. These differences could warrant subgeneric rank.

The genus *Crataegus* consists of between 140 and 200 species of hawthorn of which three large groupings stand out. First is section *Crataegus*, a group of perhaps 30 species with mainly small, usually deeply dissected leaves that possess veins to the sinuses, 20 stamens, and thorns of indeterminate growth. *Crataegus monogyna* is the commonest species in this group. Second is section *Sanguineae* with about 15 species mainly in East Asia and several species in central Asia or extending to the borders of European Russia as well as a further species in central Europe. *Crataegus nigra*, *C. sanguinea*, and *C. wilsonii* are typical of this group. These hawthorns generally have larger, more shallowly lobed leaves which, if veined to sinuses, are only veined to deep sinuses near the base of the leaf; they also have 20 stamens, laterally eroded nutlets, and short determinate thorns. Third is section *Coccineae* with shallowly lobed leaves, never any veins to the sinuses on short-shoot leaves, generally longer determinate thorns, either 10 or 20 stamens, and laterally smooth nutlets. Most of the North American species, perhaps 100 in all, belong here. *Crataegus mollis* and *C. pruinosa* are representative. In addition to the three main groupings are numerous smaller groups with a total of perhaps 20 species that partake of characters of two of the others, or are quite distinct in some way. Some of these, like *C. crus-galli*, have nearly entire-margined leaves. (See appendix 3 for a summary of these identification groups and of the medlars.)

Because the relationships of these three larger groups with each other and with the smaller groups are mainly not precisely worked out, a formal classification involving them is not attempted. Rather, about 40 small, relatively homogenous groups generally called "series" (but by some "sections") are generally recognized. If series and sections are both used then "section" is the more inclusive rank. The resultant synopsis is adumbrated in appendix 2, which is based on the listing in Phipps et al. (1990) as modified by later publications.

IDENTIFICATION. While the two medlar species are very easy to distinguish, the numerous hawthorn species are usually far less distinct from one another and much more difficult to identify. This problem is a frequent characteristic of large genera, of course. Also it appears that members of section *Crataegus* are very prone to hybridization and hybrids may be quite commonly encountered in Europe and West Asia. In North America, numerous putative hybrids within section *Coccineae* exist, but so far only two proven cases of natural hybridization are known, and, interestingly, both involve *C. monogyna* (section *Crataegus*). The North American putative hybrids are on the whole very rare, however. Hybridization obviously increases the difficulty of accurate identification.

Experience demonstrates that many hawthorns are difficult to identify and, regrettably, many published taxonomic treatments, especially in North America, are quite defective. Herbarium and arboretum specimens are often misnamed. It was not for nothing that Palmer (1932) wrote of "the *Crataegus* problem," a phrase taken up by Camp (1942) who called the genus "a veritable witches' brew." Unfortunately this problem persists, even after the passage of 70 years since Palmer, and has no easy answer. "Learning" *Crataegus* takes many years and a book such as this, which only deals with a sample of species and is primarily aimed at the enlightened horticultural market, is not the place to do it. Really keen students will do one or more of the following: study named specimens in arboreta, use reliable reference literature, make their own reference collection, and/or take photographs. Large specialist arboreta such as those at Lisle, Illinois (Morton Arboretum); Jamaica Plain, Massachusetts (Arnold Arboretum of Harvard University); Kew, London, United Kingdom (Royal Botanic Gardens); Edinburgh, United Kingdom (Royal Botanic Garden); Salaspils, Riga, Latvia; and Tashkent, Uzbekistan, are among those with good, generally well-named live reference collections of *Crataegus*. It is important to master the material in the section on structure in chapter 2 of this book before proceeding to attempt to identify hawthorns. This will alert you to those points to specially look out for and traps to avoid.

The literature on hawthorn identification is of variable quality, and popular field guides should generally be avoided not only on account of their incompleteness but also for their shortage of diagnostic information. In North America works by Palmer (1950, 1952) or Seymour (1982) are good, while Lance (1995) is a nice little guide; for Mexico, Phipps (1997); for Europe, Christensen (1992) and Franco (1968); for Russia, Pojarkova (1939, now somewhat obsolete); and for eastern Asia, Yü and Ku (1974, in Chinese) may be consulted. Identification obviously cannot be guaranteed with works that are incomplete, such as this and most garden floras (for example, Rehder 1940, Knees and Warwick 1995), although incomplete works may be adequate for plants already in general cultivation. For wild-collected material it is essential to use a treatment at a minimum complete for the region where the plant was found. There are many critical short papers in the primary literature by hawthorn specialists, but users of this book may find them over-technical. My own monograph on *Crataegus* and *Mespilus*, in preparation and due to be published within a year or two, will constitute the only comprehensive treatment for the whole world of hawthorns and medlars.

Persons wanting to study wild hawthorns and medlars are encouraged to make reference herbarium specimens (appendix 1) and identify them with the technical literature or send high quality duplicate herbarium specimens to reputable herbaria for identification. This is by far the most preferred method if one aims eventually for a high degree of accuracy. Herbarium specimens can be, with value, supplemented by close-up photography of the flowers, fruit, and foliage. Fairly fast film (ASA 200) is recommended because of frequent poor light or wind movement in the field. Use of a tripod to steady the camera is highly recommended. The difficult-to-achieve combination of fast shutter speed and small aperture is ideal to stop movement and obtain good depth of field. Otherwise use flash or remove the specimen to a well-lit spot without air movement. Although photographs are attractive and informative, good quality herbarium specimens will always preserve more information excepting true color.

The accurate identification of hawthorns on one's own is not particularly easy and is impossible without access to the appropriate literature, as discussed above. Good quality specimens, nevertheless, are usually identifiable, with a lot of care. During identification it is necessary to critically observe the many characteristics of flower, fruit, leaf shape and venation pattern, thorn and bark type, hairiness and/or glandularity of parts that exist. This, and its associated technical vocabulary (chapter 2 and glossary), can readily be mastered by anyone wishing to make the effort. Here follow a few tips. Have available a ×10 hand lens or a binocular-dissecting microscope for seeing small details such as hairs. Hairiness, if not easily visible, can also usually easily be detected by running the tongue over the surface in question against the lie of the hairs (care, if pesticides or other poisons are in use). The leaves described in this book are typical short-shoot leaves, not extension-shoot leaves which are often of different form. Mark trees of interest with a permanent tag or flag with colored tape and obtain specimens at both full flower and ripe fruit (other times will prove difficult or impossible to identify). Record color of fresh anthers and/or fully ripe fruit. Remember that common species are usually somewhat variable so that slight differences between specimens do not usually warrant a different ID. Learn to use a dichotomous key.

Users of this book will be able to make probable identifications by using the species descriptions (chapters 7 and 8) supported by the tabular key (appendix 3) and the photographs.

CHAPTER 7

Hawthorns

THERE ARE perhaps 140 species of *Crataegus* in the world, arranged in 40 series, as explained in chapter 6. This book deals with those of greatest interest to horticulturists. First, there are those generally in commerce in Britain and the United States. It is perhaps significant how few these are. Second, there is a selection of wild species seldom or never cultivated outside botanic gardens and arboreta that might consist of welcome additions to the list of generally cultivated forms. Some of these latter are merely unknown to the horticultural industry or out of fashion, others have been tried but have defects that may or may not be easily managed by careful cultivation. The reasons for this are alluded to in chapters 4 and 5. All of these, at their best, are, in my opinion, highly worthy of cultivation.

This chapter covers 69 wild and hybridogenous species and their more commonly available cultivars. Of these species, *Crataegus azarolus*, *C. mexicana*, *C. pinnatifida*, and the Mayhaws (series *Aestivales*) are all important minor fruits. Ornamental cultivars are only known from six species of hawthorn, and fruit cultivars, much more numerous, also from six species. A few ornamental cultivars are commonly grown where the species are adapted but most are not. In raising the total number of species discussed to 69 I am going beyond the totals of earlier works that dealt with *Crataegus* in an overt attempt to sell the genus on its considerable ornamental merits. This, however, will backfire if not supported by successful cultural regimens.

The basic species, or sometimes series, are arranged alphabetically in this chapter, followed by the hybrid species. Cultivars are placed with their species. The information on champion trees is taken from the *National Register of Big Trees* (American Forestry Association Staff 1999). See appendix 3 for a key to the diagnostic characteristics of the forms indicated.

HAWTHORN SPECIES

Series Aestivales (Sargent ex C. K. Schneider) Rehder
    Mayhaws
    Plates 15, 16

The Mayhaws are very distinctive large shrubs or small trees of wet places (sinkhole margins, ditches, swamp margins, river- and creeksides) along the American Gulf Coast and north into Virginia. They are characterized by short, straight thorns; unlobed or shallowly lobed small leaves; few-flowered and very early, even precocious, inflorescences; and subglobose, usually red, very early fruit. They are not very hardy, with a maximum tolerance of zone 6 (selected forms only). Their more usual range is zones 7–10.

There are two main species, western Mayhaw (*Crataegus opaca* Hooker & Arnott) from east Texas to Alabama and eastern Mayhaw (*C. aestivalis* (Walter) Torrey & A. Gray) from eastern Alabama to central Florida and Virginia. Their commercial and ornamental characteristics are essentially similar, but *C. opaca* may be distinguished by its somewhat matte, scabrous-hairy, wavy-margined leaves and *C. aestivalis* by its more *crus-galli*-like, shiny, nearly glabrous, bright green leaves with crenate margins. The U.S. National Champion for 1998, reported under the name *C. aestivalis*, which does not occur west of the Mississippi, is a *C. opaca* and comes from Angelina National Forest, Texas, where it was 13 m high in 1993.

The name "Mayhaw" refers to the month of fruiting, although only the southernmost forms fruit quite this early. More commonly, fruiting takes place June to early July. Mayhaws are a significant minor crop throughout the South from Texas to Georgia and are sold commercially by a number of nurseries. Small orchards now exist for fruit production though formerly fruit was usually gathered in the wild. This was most easily accomplished when it fell into standing water and floated. The fruit is used for conserves, jelly, pies, and tarts as well as wine.

Quite a number of cultivars exist, which are treated in the excellent book by Craft et al. (1996). Some of these have yellow fruit. Mayhaws are attractive for their precocious flowering and make nice small fruit trees for the yard, being loaded in late spring and early summer by copious fruit.

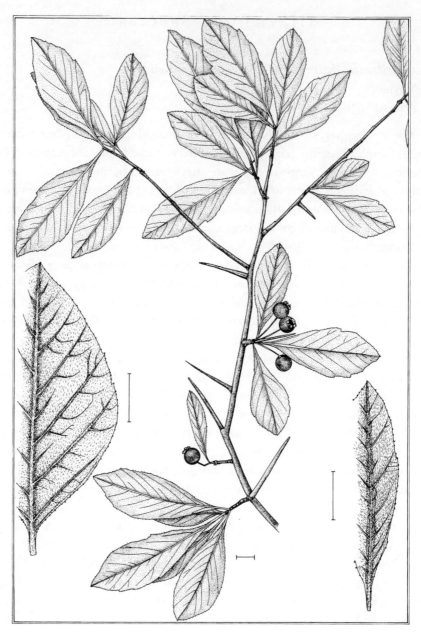

Figure 7.1. *Crataegus opaca*, western Mayhaw. Scale bars = 1 cm. Artist Susan Laurie-Bourque. Previously appeared in *Journal of the Arnold Arboretum* 69: 413 (1988). Reprinted with permission of the President and Fellows of Harvard University ©.

Plate 1. Glastonbury thorn, flowers and fruit, December 1998. Glastonbury, Somerset, United Kingdom. (photo J. B. Phipps)

Plate 2. Glastonbury thorn on Wearyall Hill, Glastonbury, Somerset, United Kingdom. (photo J. B. Phipps)

Plate 3. Peaceful late afternoon scene at Saltwells Nature Reserve, with Alan Harris, former assistant warden, looking out over pasture backed by trees and flowering wild *Crataegus monogyna*. Saltwells, West Midlands, United Kingdom. This is also the location for wild English Glastonbury thorn. (photo A. Harris)

Plate 4. Cutting the Glastonbury thorn. A schoolchild cuts flowering branches as town officials watch in an annual December ritual at Glastonbury, Somerset, United Kingdom. (photo J. B. Phipps)

Plate 5. A specimen of *Crataegus macrosperma*, eastern hawthorn, topiarized by cattle in a high-altitude pasture. Henderson County, North Carolina, United States. (photo R. W. Lance)

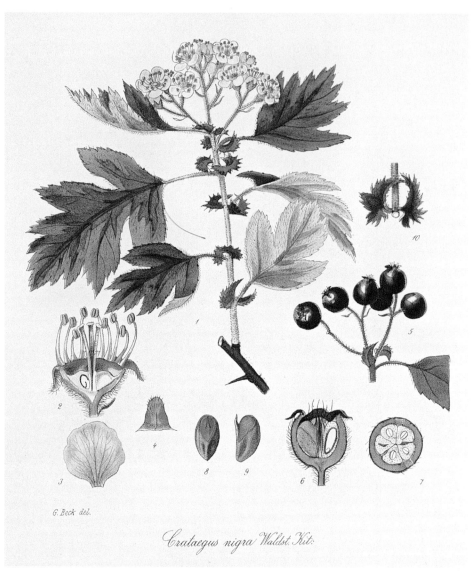

G. Beck del.

Crataegus nigra Waldst. Kit.

Plate 6. *Crataegus nigra*, Danubian hawthorn, fruit and flower dissections. 1: Several-flowered inflorescence terminal on stem; leaves and lower inflorescence branches subtended by stipules; bracteoles present along inflorescence branches. 2: Vertical section of flower showing two carpels (palest green), one with ovules, this enclosed in hypanthium tissue (darker green), three of five styles exserted through disc, nine stamens in an approximate half flower, bracteole subtending half flower. 3: Petal. 4: Sepal. 5: Infructescence with subtending stipule and foliar leaf. 6: Vertical section of fruit showing two nutlets (light brown), one with seed sectioned (white), hypanthium dark green, the whole topped by calyx lobes (black). 7: Cross-section of fruit showing pale brown bony pyrenes (nutlets), each containing seeds (white), all surrounded by hypanthial tissue (olive). 8, 9: Pyrenes shown with old style bases. 10: Leaf base with paired stipules. From Reichenbach and Reichenbach (1903).

Plate 7. Women gathering fruit of *Crataegus greggiana* for food near General Cépeda, Coahuila, Mexico. (photo J. B. Phipps; with permission, Botanical Research Institute of Texas)

Plate 8. Typical hawthorn bark is fibrous shredding with orange tones on the newly exposed surfaces, as seen here on *Crataegus gattingeri*. Alabama, United States. (photo J. B. Phipps)

Plate 9. The bark of a few hawthorn species exfoliates in large thin flakes to reveal a smooth surface, as seen here on *Crataegus spathulata*, littlehip hawthorn. Chattahoochee River, Georgia, United States. (photo J. B. Phipps)

Plate 10. Ancient field pattern in west England showing use of hedgerows for boundaries. View west from Long Mynd, Shropshire, United Kingdom. (photo J. B. Phipps)

Plate 11. A freshly laid hawthorn hedge, with trimmed lumber for uprights. Natural uprights can also be used. Shropshire, United Kingdom. (photo B. G. Tromans)

Plate 12. A laid hawthorn hedge maintained by mechanical trimming. Shropshire, United Kingdom. (photo J. B. Phipps)

Plate 13. *Crataegus* sp. aff. *C. chrysocarpa*, in brilliant fruit. Also note, some rust may be observed on one leaf, top right. Near Missoula, Montana, United States (photo J. B. Phipps)

Plate 14. Occasionally the mainly white flowers of wild *Crataegus* ×*gravis* are brilliantly flecked blood-red. Southern Ontario, Canada. (photo J. B. Phipps)

Plate 15. *Crataegus aestivalis*, eastern Mayhaw. A red-fruited cultivated plant in Louisiana, United States. (photo G. Melcher)

Plate 16. *Crataegus opaca*, western Mayhaw. A yellow-fruited cultivated plant in Louisiana, United States. (photo G. Melcher)

Plate 17. *Crataegus aprica*, sunny hawthorn. Fruiting branches of a cultivated bush in Kew, United Kingdom. Unripe fruit is an attractive apricot-orange. (photo K. R. Robertson)

Plate 18. *Crataegus brachyacantha*, blueberry haw. The fruit looks like blueberry, though it often changes to black later. From a cultivated plant at the University of North Carolina Arboretum, Asheville, North Carolina, United States. (photo R. W. Lance)

Plate 19. *Crataegus calpodendron*, late hawthorn. A flowering branch. Southern Ontario, Canada. (photo J. B. Phipps)

Plate 20. *Crataegus calpodendron*, late hawthorn. Fruiting branches. Southern Ontario, Canada. (photo J. B. Phipps)

Plate 21. *Crataegus coccinea*, scarlet hawthorn. A fully laden bush. Ontario, Canada. (photo J. B. Phipps)

Plate 22. *Crataegus coccinioides*, Kansas hawthorn. A fruiting branch. Well-grown, this species is one of the most handsome hawthorns. (photo J. B. Phipps)

Plate 23. *Crataegus crus-galli*, cockspur hawthorn. A fruiting branch of a selected form cultivated in Boulder, Colorado, United States. (photo J. B. Phipps)

Plate 24. *Crataegus crus-galli*, cockspur hawthorn. A fruiting branch. Southwestern Ontario, Canada. (photo J. B. Phipps)

Plate 25. *Crataegus crus-galli*, cockspur hawthorn. A flowering bush showing typical layered branching. This is the *C. tenax* form with 20 stamens. London Township, Middlesex County, Ontario, Canada. (photo J. B. Phipps)

Plate 26. *Crataegus douglasii*, Douglas hawthorn, and *C. okennonii*, O'Kennon hawthorn. Branches intermixed (*C. douglasii* is black and bloomy). Northern Okanagan, British Columbia, Canada. (photo J. B. Phipps)

Plate 27. *Crataegus lacrimata*, weeping hawthorn. Flowering bushes. Florida panhandle, United States. (photo J. B. Phipps)

Plate 28. *Crataegus* ser. *Lacrimatae*, weeping hawthorn. A fruiting shoot. Florida, United States. (photo J. B. Phipps)

Plate 29. *Crataegus laevigata* 'François Rigaud', woodland hawthorn. A rare yellow-fruited form that is quite attractive. Kew, United Kingdom. (photo R. J. O'Kennon)

Plate 30. *Crataegus laevigata* 'Gireoudii', woodland hawthorn. A strikingly heavy crop of large handsome fruit. Kew, United Kingdom. (photo J. B. Phipps)

Plate 31. *Crataegus macrosperma*, eastern hawthorn. A fruiting branch. Southern Ontario, Canada. (photo J. B. Phipps)

Plate 32. *Crataegus marshallii*, parsley haw. A flowering branch. The abundant flowers, bright rose-red anthers, and delicate foliage make this species very attractive. Arkansas, United States. (photo J. B. Phipps)

Plate 33. *Crataegus marshallii*, parsley haw. A fruiting branch. Arkansas, United States. (photo J. B. Phipps)

Plate 34. *Crataegus ×media* 'Paul's Scarlet'. A tree in full bloom. Shropshire, United Kingdom. (photo B. G. Tromans)

Plate 35. *Crataegus ×media* 'Paul's Scarlet'. Close-up of flowers. Shropshire, United Kingdom. (photo B. G. Tromans)

Plate 36. *Crataegus ×media* 'Punicea'. A cultivated plant. Kew, United Kingdom. (photo K. R. Robertson)

Plate 37. *Crataegus ×media* 'Rubra Plena'. A cultivated plant. North of Salt Lake City, Utah, United States. (photo J. B. Phipps)

Plate 38. *Crataegus mexicana*, tejocote. Yellow-colored fruit with U.S. coins for comparison. Purchased in local market, Veracruz State, Mexico. (photo K. R. Robertson).

Plate 39. *Crataegus mexicana*, tejocote. A fruiting branch of the copper-colored form. Hidalgo State, Mexico. (photo R. J. O'Kennon).

Plate 40. *Crataegus mexicana*, tejocote. Clonal stock as grown in Puebla State, Mexico. With author, 1985. (photo J. B. Phipps)

Plate 41. *Crataegus monogyna*, one-seeded hawthorn. A 10.6-m flowering tree. Saltwells Nature Reserve, West Midlands, United Kingdom. (photo A. Harris)

Plate 42. *Crataegus monogyna*, one-seeded hawthorn. Fruit is usually, however, a duller oxblood-red. From a cultivated plant, Royal Botanic Gardens, Kew, United Kingdom. (photo K. R. Robertson)

Plate 43. *Crataegus monogyna* 'Crimson Cloud', one-seeded hawthorn. A cultivated plant. Ailsa Craig, Ontario, Canada. (photo J. B. Phipps)

Plate 44. *Crataegus okanaganensis*, Okanagan hawthorn. Fruit color mid to late August. Northern Okanagan, British Columbia, Canada. (photo J. B. Phipps, permission of Botanical Research Institute of Texas)

Plate 45. *Crataegus okennonii*, O'Kennon hawthorn. Fruiting branches in mid to late August. Northern Okanagan, British Columbia, Canada. (photo R. J. O'Kennon)

Plate 46. *Crataegus orientalis*, oriental hawthorn. Fruit of a plant in the Royal Botanic Garden, Edinburgh, United Kingdom. (photo J. B. Phipps)

Plate 47. *Crataegus schraderiana*. Fruit of a plant in Hillier Arboretum, United Kingdom. This species is apparently a form of *C. orientalis*. (photo J. B. Phipps)

Plate 48. *Crataegus pentagyna*, small-flowered black hawthorn. A fruiting branch. Kew, United Kingdom. (photo R. J. O'Kennon)

Plate 49. *Crataegus phaenopyrum*, Washington thorn. Fruit and beautiful fall foliage color on a cultivated plant. Ailsa Craig, Ontario, Canada. (photo J. B. Phipps)

Plate 50. *Crataegus phippsii*, Phipps hawthorn. Fruit in mid to late September. Northern Okanagan, British Columbia, Canada. This species is one of a small group of recently discovered hawthorns that ripen to this somewhat unusual color. (photo R. J. O'Kennon)

Plate 51. *Crataegus pinnatifida* var. *major*. A fruiting bush. Cultivated at Morton Arboretum, Illinois, United States. (photo Morton Arboretum)

Plate 52. *Crataegus pruinosa*, frosted hawthorn. A flowering branch. Ontario, Canada. (photo J. B. Phipps)

Plate 53. *Crataegus pruinosa*, frosted hawthorn. A fruiting branch. Southern Ontario, Canada. (photo J. B. Phipps)

Plate 54. *Crataegus punctata*, white haw. A fruiting branch of the common burgundy-colored form. Ontario, Canada. (photo J. B. Phipps)

Plate 55. *Crataegus punctata*, white haw. Early spring scene showing large numbers of the well-named white haw. Along the Ausable River, near Lucan, Ontario, Canada. (photo J. B. Phipps)

Plate 56. *Crataegus rivularis*, river hawthorn. A fruiting branch. The fruit of this handsome species changes from burgundy (mid to late August) to black when fully ripe. Utah, United States. (photo R. J. O'Kennon)

Plate 57. *Crataegus spathulata*, littlehip hawthorn. A fruiting branch. Alabama, United States. (photo J. B. Phipps)

Plate 58. *Crataegus succulenta* var. *occidentalis*, succulent hawthorn. A typical wild form from western range of species. Not quite ripe fruit is an attractive shade of reddish orange. Washington, United States. (photo J. B. Phipps)

Plate 59. *Crataegus succulenta* var. *occidentalis*, succulent hawthorn. Ripe fruit. Northwestern Montana, United States. (photo J. B. Phipps)

Plate 60. *Crataegus ?succulenta*, succulent hawthorn. An exquisitely beautiful form growing near the Illyria Hotel, Ljubljana, Slovenia. (photo J. B. Phipps)

Plate 61. *Crataegus tracyi*, Tracy hawthorn. A fruiting branch from a plant growing in the mountains of Coahuila, Mexico. (photo J. B. Phipps)

Plate 62. *Crataegus aurescens*. This close relative of *C. tracyi* has the most beautiful yellow to orange fruit, the two colors often seen at the same time, but the plant is not very hardy. Coahuila, Mexico. (photo J. B. Phipps)

Plate 63. *Crataegus triflora*, three-flowered hawthorn. Extremely large (for a hawthorn) white flowers and multiple stems like those of the beauty bush, *Kolkwitzia*, are features of this plant. Though rarely cultivated, this hawthorn is outstanding when well-grown. Alabama, United States. (photo J. B. Phipps)

Plate 64. *Crataegus uniflora*, one-flowered hawthorn. A flowering shoot. This species flowers while still very small. Georgia, United States. (photo J. B. Phipps)

Plate 65. *Crataegus ×vailiae*, Vail's hawthorn. Fruiting branches. Kew, United Kingdom. (photo K. R. Robertson)

Plate 66. *Crataegus viridis* 'Winter King', green hawthorn. Flowers and fruit from a cultivated plant. Tennessee, United States. (photo J. B. Phipps)

Plate 67. *Crataegus wilsonii*, Wilson's hawthorn. Beautiful, wrinkled, mature leaves act as a perfect foil for the glossy scarlet fruit. Kew, United Kingdom. (photo K. R. Robertson)

Plate 68. *Crataegus* ×*grignonensis*, Grignon hawthorn. A fruiting branch. Thornhayes Nursery, Devonshire, United Kingdom. (photo K. Croucher)

Plate 69. *Crataegus* ×*lavallei*, Lavallée hawthorn. Beautiful white flowers and deep green foliage will give way to soft apricot-colored fruit, changing to orange, yellow, and red. A cultivated plant. Ailsa Craig, Ontario, Canada. (photo J. B. Phipps)

Plate 70. *Crataegus* ×*mordenensis* 'Toba', Morden hawthorn. Fruit from a cultivated plant. Coldstream, British Columbia, Canada. (photo J. B. Phipps)

Plate 71. *Crataegus* ×*persimilis*, plumleaf hawthorn. Developing autumn color. Kew, United Kingdom. (photo R. J. O'Kennon)

Plate 72. *Mespilus canescens*, Stern's medlar. Bright scarlet but somewhat sparingly produced fruit of a cultivated plant. St. Louis, Missouri, United States. (photo J. B. Phipps)

Plate 73. *Mespilus canescens*, Stern's medlar. A flowering bush, with (left to right) unknown; William Shepherd, Arkansas Natural Heritage Commission; unknown; unknown; Mrs. and Mr. Sam Konecny, landowners; unknown; J. B. Phipps; Jane Stern, discoverer; and R. J. O'Kennon. Arkansas, United States. (photo J. B. Phipps)

Plate 74. *Mespilus germanica*, common medlar. Fruit of a cultivated plant. Hungary. (photo J. B. Phipps)

Plate 75. ×*Crataemespilus grandiflora*, medlar-hawthorn. Fruiting branches. As the season progresses the fruit will ripen to burgundy and the leaves turn yellow, making a very attractive combination. Kew, United Kingdom. (photo J. B. Phipps)

Crataegus aprica Beadle
sunny hawthorn
Plate 17

Crataegus aprica is generally a small to medium-sized bush, rather dense and twiggy, with short, straight thorns and broad-elliptic, unlobed or barely lobed leaves bordered by small gland-tipped teeth. The inflorescences are few-flowered and followed by globose red or reddish-orange fruit containing 4–5 nutlets. The sunny hawthorn is a plant of southern Appalachia to the Florida panhandle where it is quite common. It is mainly found in open brushy habitats and in nature occurs in zones 7–9. The group of species to which *C. aprica* belongs (series *Flavae*) is not normally cultivated outside botanical gardens and arboreta, but this species can be highly recommended as an ornamental, where well suited and when well grown, for its compact habit, pretty flowers, small leaves, and reddish, quite large fruit.

Cratageus azarolus Linnaeus
azarole

The azarole is a large bush or small tree bearing indeterminate thorns and smallish, deeply lobed, gray-hairy leaves with veins to the sinuses. The fruit varies in color from yellow to orange-red or rarely whitish and usually has 2–3 nutlets. *Crataegus azarolus* is native to the central and eastern Mediterranean and does not occur naturally at its western end. It is also found through Turkey and Iran to Kyrgyzstan. Its natural habitat is maquis or open woodland. It grows best in zones 7–10, being especially suited for areas with a longish and somewhat dry summer. The azarole has become a minor fruit, and fruit sizes up to 3 cm in diameter have been recorded. The kinds cultivated for fruits (var. *azarolus*, var. *chlorocarpa*) are taller and less thorny bushes than the wild forms (var. *aronia*, var. *pontica*). The azarole makes an excellent ornamental when well-suited particularly if the bright vermillion-fruited kind can be obtained. An excellent illustration of this species may be found by Beck in Reichenbach and Reichenbach (1903).

Crataegus brachyacantha Sargent & Engelmann
blueberry haw
Plate 18

Crataegus brachyacantha is a large shrub or small tree to 10 m with very short, usually recurved thorns. The leaves are more or less elliptic, unlobed, glossy, with cre-

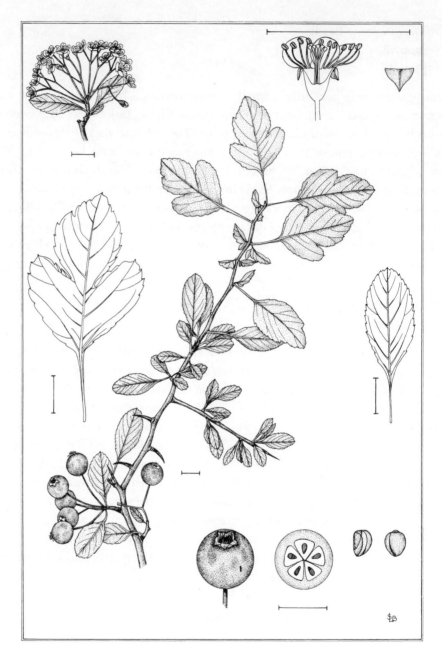

Figure 7.2. *Crataegus brachyacantha*, blueberry haw. Scale bars = 1 cm. Artist Susan Laurie-Bourque. Previously appeared in *Annals of the Missouri Botanical Garden* 85: 489 (1998). Reprinted with permission of the journal ©.

nate margins, and fairly small. The flowers are numerous, small, in a domed inflorescence, and turn yellow-orange at late maturity. The fruit is subglobose, containing 5 nutlets, eventually dead black, but earlier deep purple overlaid by a conspicuous bloom. Blueberry haw is found in the United States throughout Louisiana and just enters each of the neighboring states. It grows best in damp alluvial soils and is hardy in zones 7–11. The U.S. National Champion in 1998 was 11 m tall in 1993 and comes from Nacogdoches Company, Texas. Sargent (1890), however, recorded a maximum height of 15 m. The fruit is not as pleasant to the taste as the common name would suggest, which only refers to the appearance, for the flesh is thin and, to the palate, dry or slightly bitter.

This species is rarely cultivated yet has great potential as an ornamental. The handsome glossy foliage colors brilliantly in fall to shades of crimson, scarlet, burnished copper, and yellow. The fruit is reliably handsome when covered by bloom and black later while the flowers turn from white to an interesting orange-yellow when old, a feature shared by only a few other hawthorns. Long ago Palmer described a white-fruited form, f. *albiflora*, from near Nachitoches, Louisiana, which has not been seen since. This constitutes the only record of a white-fruited hawthorn and its rediscovery would be of great horticultural interest.

Crataegus calpodendron (Ehrhart) Medikus
late hawthorn
Plates 19, 20

Late hawthorn is a large shrub or small tree with generally few (even no) thorns that are usually 3–4 cm long, stout, straight or more or less recurved. The leaf blades are usually rhombic or rhombic-ovate with roughly lobed, serrate margins. The numerous small flowers have 20 stamens with usually reddish anthers and are followed by smallish globose or ellipsoid orange-red fruit with usually 2–3 nutlets.

Crataegus calpodendron ranges widely through the eastern United States and adjacent southern Canada. Northwards it is a plant of open scrubby places and southwards of woodland understory. Details of leaf shape are very variable. The species is found naturally in zones 5–9. The U.S. National Champion for 1998 came from Pope, Illinois, and was 6 m tall in 1971. I have seen somewhat taller trees in Alabama.

Ornamentally, perhaps only the northern forms are worth considering, especially for their unusual arching habit of growth (southern woodland forms are erect). This species flowers second latest of all North American hawthorns (*Cratae-

gus phaenopyrum is last), in mid-June in the North. The fruit is attractive, but it is a challenge to keep good foliage through the summer and there is no fall color to speak of.

Crataegus chlorosarca Maximowicz

Crataegus chlorosarca is generally a large bush or small tree 6 m tall with short (2–3 cm) determinate thorns, else thornless. It has more or less ovate to narrow-ovate multiveined (8–10 veins) leaves with shallow sinuses, small flowers, and, at full ripeness, round, black fruit. The plant parts are fairly hairy. The species is found in northeast Asia in Manchuria, adjacent Siberia, and northern Japan in forest edges and openings as well as streamsides. This hawthorn is rarely cultivated, but it forms a handsome specimen in British botanical gardens and arboreta. Pojarkova (1939) also recommended it as an excellent ornamental. It is probably hardy to zone 4 or even 3.

The related *Crataegus nigra* Waldstein & Kitaibel ex Willdenow (Plate 6) from central Europe appears to be a much inferior ornamental, while the related and more or less glabrous *C. jozana* C. K. Schneider from northeast Asia is probably as good as *C. chlorosarca*.

Crataegus chrysocarpa Ashe
fireberry hawthorn
synonym *C. columbiana* Howell, in the sense of American authors

Crataegus chrysocarpa is a shrub usually 2–3 m tall, very thorny, with ovate to rhombic, usually quite sharply lobed, generally smallish leaves. The flowers are 8–10 to the inflorescence and fairly early. The fruit is generally suborbicular, hairy, bright red or reddish at maturity, with usually 3–4 nutlets. The species is the second most widespread hawthorn in North America nearly reaching the Pacific from Oregon to southern interior British Columbia whence it ranges on both sides of the Canada–U.S. border to Newfoundland and Maine. It is a plant of scrubby places in the East and mainly in draws and along watercourses in the prairies and intermontane regions.

Crataegus chrysocarpa is very variable, mainly in details of leaf shape and pubescence, as befits so common a species. It is sometimes called goldenberry hawthorn in the literature, but this misnomer is merely a translation of Ashe's poorly chosen scientific name. Western forms are, however, an attractive salmon-orange in fruit at one stage of the ripening process, previous to which they may be yellowish green or rarely golden. In my view it is not generally helpful to name a species after its unripe fruit.

Fireberry hawthorn is seldom used as an ornamental but has value for landscaping in northern regions, where few other species are hardy, particularly if it can be protected from drought. The bright deep green foliage is a fine foil for the red fruit in well-grown material. West of the Rocky Mountains superb autumnal colors of yellow may be observed. The plant portrayed in Plate 13 resembles these forms but is probably not *Crataegus chrysocarpa*. Some western forms should also be extremely drought resistant. Plants from northern Ontario must be cold-hardy to at least zone 2.

Crataegus coccinea Linnaeus
scarlet hawthorn
Plate 21

Crataegus coccinea is a large shrub or small tree generally 5–10 m tall, with stout thorns and large, more or less ovate, shallowly but sharply lobed leaves. The medium-sized flowers are fairly early and are followed by large, orbicular, scarlet fruit containing usually 4–5 nutlets. Scarlet hawthorn is distributed throughout the southern Great Lakes region to New England and south in the Appalachian chain to North Carolina. Through much of this area it is rather common, occurring along fence lines and in old pastures and woodland margins. It is found in zones 5–6. The U.S. National Champion was 11.2 m tall in 1980 and came from Oneida, New York. Well-grown, this species is one of the finest ornamentals in the genus and it can bear totally spectacular crops of scarlet fruit. The foliage of better forms colors well to a nice yellow and gold and could, with advantage, be carefully sought out. It is widely planted in London, United Kingdom (Wurzell 1992).

Crataegus pringlei Sargent (synonym *C. coccinea* var. *pringlei* (Sargent) Macklin & J. B. Phipps) is closely related and has conspicuously convex foliage more likely to be nearly equally tapered to both ends and a more oblong fruit. It has nearly the same distribution and is equally as good an ornamental.

Crataegus holmesiana Ashe, with more elongated fruit and leaves, is also similar and in its best (anthocyanin-rich when young) forms could also make an excellent ornamental.

Crataegus coccinioides Ashe
Kansas hawthorn
synonym *C. dilatata* Sargent
Plate 22

Crataegus coccinioides is a very thorny large bush or small tree with large, more or less ovate, shallowly lobed leaves. The large flowers are fairly early and are followed by medium-sized, subglobose, bright pinkish-red to scarlet or crimson fruit with generally 5 nutlets. Kansas hawthorn ranges from Kansas to southern New England just entering southern Canada. It occurs in brushy places, fence lines, woodland edges, and so forth and thrives in zones 5–6. The U.S. National Champion for 1998 was 9 m tall in 1972 and grew in the Brooklyn Botanic Gardens, New York. It is a very variable species, ranging from more or less glabrous to densely hairy.

As an ornamental, well-grown Kansas hawthorn is among the most striking American species. Its large flowers and leaves, fairly large and unusually brilliantly colored fruit, together with some autumnal foliage color can add up to a great effect. The highly attractive deep rose-pink color of the fruit is caused by a heavy bloom, which, if rubbed off, reveals an equally ornamental but more commonplace bright red color.

Crataegus crus-galli Linnaeus
cockspur hawthorn
synonym *C. tenax* Ashe
Plates 23, 24, 25

Crataegus crus-galli is generally a very dense bush to small tree to 10 m tall usually with characteristic layered branching. The thorns are numerous and often large, and the leaves lack lobes, are very glossy, and are usually deep green with fine marginal teeth. The fairly large inflorescences appear in mid-season and are followed by subglobose to more or less oblong fruit usually of some shade of red and containing 1–3 nutlets.

Cockspur hawthorn occurs nearly throughout the eastern half of the United States and is often common in the wild. It is generally found in full light situations and does not seem to tolerate shade in the manner of many southern hawthorns. Plants from northern provenances are hardy to zone 4, but the most southern forms are probably not hardy above zone 7. This species is very variable as befits something so common, and careful selection could be made from the wild for forms well-adapted to particular regions. The subtle variations in leaf shape, hairiness, tone of green, and fruit color not to mention the existence of rare yellow-fruited forms could spark a bonanza for the plant hunter. Some forms also color very well in the fall.

As an ornamental *Crataegus crus-galli* is one of the best hawthorns, with its smart, glossy, green foliage often arranged in seried ranks, its abundant flower and fruit, and its moderate drought tolerance. Thornless forms are known but in itself this would seem to confer little benefit outside the nursery. This is one of the few *Crataegus* species reasonably well-established in the horticultural trade and wider use of the many attractive variants would be sensible. Unfortunately, few nursery-men seriously venture into the wild.

Crataegus tenax Ashe is a 20-stamen form, otherwise indistinguishable.

Crataegus engelmannii Sargent (? synonym *C. berberifolia* Torrey & A. Gray) is often segregated as the very hairy form of *C. crus-galli* and differs little in essentials from *C. rosei* of the Sierras Madre Oriental and Occidental of Mexico.

Crataegus reverchonii Sargent represents a southwestern (Texas, Oklahoma) form with slightly different leaf shape and much greater drought tolerance.

Crataegus fecunda Sargent from Missouri to Illinois, Ohio, and Arkansas is a distinctive form with very large fruit and brilliantly colored autumn foliage (Sargent 1902). It cannot now be found in the wild.

Crataegus cuneata Siebold & Zuccarini
cuneate hawthorn, shan li hung

This small (perhaps multistemmed) bush is at most 2 or 3 m tall, probably with arching branches in the larger forms (described as scandent by one collector). The twigs are unarmed or with more or less numerous short, somewhat fine, aphyllous thorns 0.5–1.0 cm long. Thorn-tipped shoots may grow out in this species, and the thorns are therefore in reality indeterminate. The small leaves vary from quite entire (*Crataegus tangchungchangii* F. P. Metcalf form) to deeply trilobed (like some forms of *C. spathulata*). Where lobed, the leaves are veined to the sinuses. Leaf shapes intermediate between these extremes are the most common. Vegetative parts are generally densely pubescent to tomentose, especially when young. The flowers are 12–15 mm in diameter, in floriferous inflorescences with pretty red stamens. The fruit, yellow to more commonly red at full ripeness, is normally borne singly in the infructescence, is pubescent, subglobose and 10–15 mm in diameter, with 4–5 nutlets. The flesh of the fruit is green.

Crataegus cuneata is widespread in the southern half of China in brushy situations and is hardy in zones 8–11. It is hardly cultivated in the West, even in arboreta, but many herbarium specimens are so pretty that it is probably well worth growing as an ornamental in appropriate climates. A specimen from Hunan Province had deep rose flowers quite different from the faded pink of older flowers of many *Crataegus*. This would be well worth relocating if possible. Cuneate hawthorn is cultivated for its fruit in China and Japan.

Crataegus douglasii Lindley
Douglas hawthorn
Plate 26

Crataegus douglasii is a medium-sized to large bush with reddish-brown or orange-brown bark on 2- to 5-cm thick twigs. It has short, 2- to 3-cm long, slightly recurved thorns. The shallowly lobed, broad-elliptic to obovate leaves are bright green in summer and generally color to yellowish copper. The small flowers are borne in tight inflorescences and are followed by normally ellipsoid black fruit that are very bloomy early and contain usually 3–4 nutlets. Douglas hawthorn is commonest in the Pacific Northwest of the United States and southern British Columbia but extends sporadically eastwards to the northern Great Lakes area. It occurs in scrubby sites and would have a maximum hardiness rating of zones 3–5 depending on provenance. Well-grown, Douglas hawthorn is a smart plant, but under dry conditions it is scrappy. I am not using the name "black hawthorn" because this can apply to other, related species. The U.S. National Champion is recorded from Beacon Rock State Park, Washington, and was 12.5 m tall in 1993. The identity of this specimen should be critically checked against other species in series *Douglasianae*.

Crataegus suksdorfii (Sargent) Kruschke, with a more Pacific distribution, is a related species with 20 stamens.

Crataegus harbisonii Beadle
Harbison hawthorn

Harbison hawthorn is a vigorous bush to 7 or 8 m with stout, medium-sized thorns that are shiny blackish at 2 years. The leaves are broad-elliptic with small but sharp lobes and are quite hairy. The inflorescence has 5–12 medium-sized flowers and is quite striking. It is followed by subglobose reddish fruit containing 3–5 nutlets.

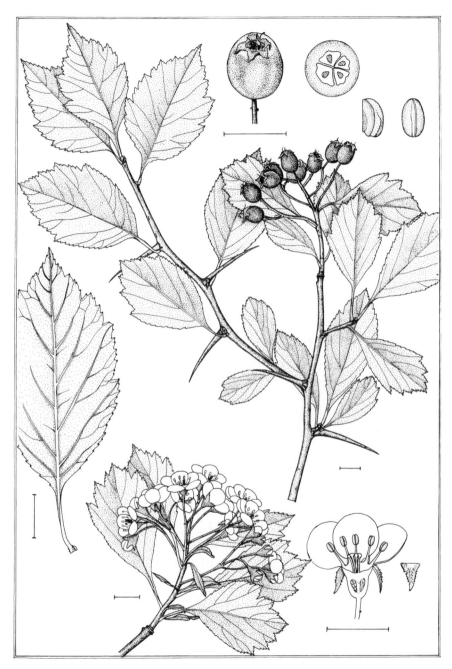

Figure 7.3. *Crataegus douglasii*, Douglas hawthorn. Bitterroot Valley form (shown here) has rather long thorns. Scale bars = 1 cm. Artist Susan Laurie-Bourque.

Crataegus harbisonii was originally described from Nashville, Tennessee, where it is apparently now extinct. It was saved by Ron W. Lance, who collected seed and sowed them at Asheville, North Carolina (see Lance and Phipps 2000). It should make a handsome ornamental, carefully grown, with its vigorous growth, firm leaves, and globular red fruit.

A related but much more widespread species, *Crataegus ashei* Beadle, is a little smaller in all its parts, with layered branching and with a distribution similar to that of *C. triflora*.

Crataegus intricata Lange
 intricate hawthorn
 including *Crataegus rubella* Beadle, *C. neobushii* Sargent

Crataegus intricata is a very thorny bush 2–5 m tall. Two-year-old thorns are more or less slender, recurved, and blackish. The leaves are more or less ovate to broad-elliptic, usually conspicuously though shallowly lobed, and more or less glabrous on both sides. Inflorescences are few-flowered, with medium-sized flowers followed by few subglobose medium-sized fruit in a variety of colors—pink, ruddy, orange, and yellow. The fruiting calyx is elevated as in *C. pruinosa* and has 3–5 nutlets. *Crataegus intricata* in the broad sense has almost exactly the same geographical distribution as *C. pruinosa*. Members of the *C. intricata* complex differ mainly in fruit color, absence of pruinosity on fruit, (sometimes much) greater hairiness (*C. biltmoreana*), and absence of tree forms southwards. The intricate hawthorn is hardy in zones 5–8. It is not cultivated outside arboreta and botanic gardens but superior forms could be interesting for the color range of the fruit.

Crataegus biltmoreana Beadle (Biltmore hawthorn) is a copiously hairy relative with much the same distribution range. A specimen, perhaps this species, from Warrenton, Virginia, is claimed to be the U.S. National champion for Biltmore hawthorn and was 7 m tall when recorded in 1982.

Series Lacrimatae J. B. Phipps
 weeping hawthorns
 Plates 27, 28

Series *Lacrimatae* are bushes or small trees to 7 m but usually much smaller and very thorny with short to medium thorns. The branchlets hang more or less vertically at their tips on mature branches and are flexuous at the nodes. The very small unlobed leaves have few lateral veins. The inflorescences are few-flowered (1–4, occasionally 5) and glabrous to tomentose. The fruit, usually borne singly, is orbicular and yellow to red, commonly a strong dull copper-orange; it contains 3–5 nutlets and ripens early, in August. Species of series *Lacrimatae* are common from Alabama to North Carolina and southwards to central Florida on sandy soils, often in pine barrens. Indeed, they constitute the only series of southeastern thorns where thousands of specimens can be seen in one location. They are probably mostly hardy in zones 6–8.

The many kinds of hawthorn in series *Lacrimatae* were mainly described by Beadle at the beginning of the 20th century and the taxonomy is only just beginning to get sorted out. Most have mistakenly been called *Crataegus flava* and *C. michauxii*, but the name *C. lacrimata* Small has been correctly used for a tall, glabrous, narrow-leaved form from northern Florida. I segregated series *Lacrimatae* from series *Flavae* in 1988 due to differences in plant habit, leaf form, and other characteristics.

These plants should be better known. They are natural xeriscape subjects, being able to tolerate extended dry periods in the summer with temperatures in the upper 30s (Celsius). They are occasionally seen in the gardens of adventurous amateurs in the region and are also occasionally offered by nurseries. *Crataegus lepida* Beadle, the smallest member of this group, flowers as late as May in central Florida and blooms when less than 1 m tall. This plant has great potential. Among the taller kinds those with the smaller leaves and thinnest twigs have the most lacrimose growth, constituting the true weeping willows of the hawthorn kingdom (Plate 27). These can be exceptionally beautiful. The stouter kinds with larger fruit, larger leaves, and thicker twigs also have much to offer to the southeastern landscapist.

Crataegus laevigata (Poiret) A.-P. de Candolle
woodland hawthorn, midland hawthorn
synonym *C. oxyacanthoides* Thuillier
Plates 29, 30

Crataegus laevigata is a large bush or small tree to 8 m. The small, very shallowly and obtusely lobed leaves are nearly glabrous with veins to the sinuses. The thorns are indeterminate, and the glabrous inflorescences bear small to medium-sized flowers, followed by red subglobose fruits with usually 2–3 nutlets. The range of this species is concentrated in central Europe where the plant is more shade tolerant than *C. monogyna*. It also flowers 1–2 weeks before *C. monogyna*. Unlike *C. monogyna*, it

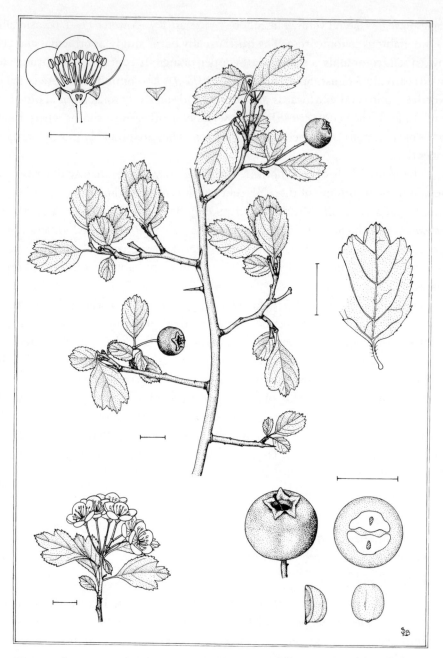

Figure 7.4. *Crataegus laevigata*, woodland hawthorn, midland hawthorn. Scale bars
= 1 cm. Artist Susan Laurie-Bourque. Previously appeared in *Canadian Journal of
Botany* 76: 1872 (1998). Reprinted with permission of the journal ©.

has few records of natural introduction to countries outside Europe. In cultivation it thrives best in zones 5–7, if sufficiently rust-free.

W oodland hawthorn can make an excellent ornamental. The wild type is worth cultivating and its best forms make a very dense shrub laden with red fruit. It has given rise to a number of interesting cultivars of which the following can be recommended.

'Aurea': Like the wild form but with bright yellow fruit. Pretty.

'François Rigaud': Like 'Aurea' but perhaps tougher. Very attractive. Plate 29.

'Gireoudii': Leaves conspicuously variegated when young, much less distinctly so, however, with age; a good crop of the bright red fruit can be extremely stunning. Plate 30.

'Rosea': Flowers single, light pink.

Most selections offered under this species are actually *Crataegus ×media*, which see.

Crataegus macrosperma Ashe
eastern hawthorn
including *C. roanensis* Ashe
Plates 5, 31

Crataegus macrosperma is a small to large bush rarely more than 5 m tall. It is usually very thorny, with stout, short-medium thorns. The leaves are more or less ovate, shallowly but sharply lobed, and covered with a fine, stiff, nearly invisible hair above. The medium-sized flowers are in medium-sized inflorescences and are followed by ellipsoid to subglobose, bright to deep red fruit containing 3–5 nutlets. The species occurs through the eastern half of the United States and adjacent Canada from Minnesota to Newfoundland south to Missouri and the southern Appalachians. It becomes much less common southwards at the lower altitudes. Found in brushy places, woodlot margins, and woodland understory (South), it is hardy in zones 5–7.

Though not a major ornamental perhaps due to shaggy plant habit, tendency to sucker, and problems with foliage in the summer, eastern hawthorn can be incredibly pretty well-grown, full of flowers in spring, and with a fine crop of scarlet to deeper red fruit in fall. Among its distinctions are the deep anthocyanins that color the young foliage—this is peculiarly beautiful in transmitted light—and its ability to tolerate shearing (see Plate 5). The U.S. National Champion of *Crataegus flabellata*, recorded from the Shenandoah National Park, Virginia, is probably *C. macrosperma* as it is well out of range for *C. flabellata*.

Crataegus schuettei Ashe, with 20 stamens (*C. macrosperma* has 5–7 or 10) is a related species of similar ornamental value.

Crataegus flabellata (Bosc ex Spach) K. Koch, restricted to the northeastern United States (not south of New York) and adjacent Canada, is another related species but one whose characteristics are intermediate between *C. macrosperma* and *C. chrysocarpa*. Compared with *C. macrosperma*, it has more sharply lobed foliage, a pubescent inflorescence, and glandular-serrate calyx lobes. *Crataegus flabellata* has generally similar landscape and ornamental qualities to *C. macrosperma*.

Crataegus marshallii Eggleston
parsley haw
Plates 32, 33

Crataegus marshallii is a large shrub or small tree to 10 m tall whose trunk bark exfoliates to a smooth surface. The thorns are few to numerous, fine, short, and determinate, and the leaves are small, deeply dissected, and deltate-ovate, with veins to sinuses. The flowers are in domed inflorescences and have reddish anthers. The fruit is small, ellipsoid, and shiny scarlet, containing 1–2 nutlets.

Parsley haw is widely distributed through the southeastern quarter of the United States and is often found in open woodland. It is obviously most closely related to the European hawthorns of section *Crataegus* even though differing in its determinate thorns. The U.S. National Champion for 1999 was measured in 1997 and stood 8.2 m high in Covington County, Mississippi.

Crataegus marshallii is a superior ornamental when well-grown, on account of its beautiful flowers, delicate foliage, smart glossy fruit, and beautiful exfoliating bark, very similar to that of *C. spathulata*. It can be considered a four-season ornamental. Specimens from northern provenances are hardy to zone 5.

Crataegus ×media Bechstein
Plates 34, 35, 36, 37

This hybrid hawthorn, generally intermediate between *Crataegus monogyna* and *C. laevigata*, can be readily found wild in Europe where both parents occur. A number of important cultivars seemingly belong here, rather than to either parent, where they are usually referred. See Geerinck (1998) for some of the fine points on cultivar nomenclature. Like its parents, *C. ×media* is hardy in zones 5–7, though cultivars usually perform rather poorly in zones 6–7 in North America, rust being

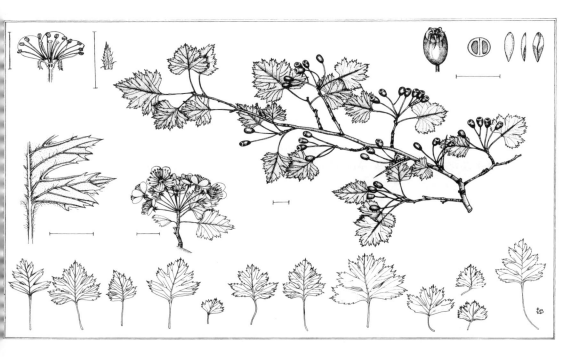

Figure 7.5. *Crataegus marshallii*, parsley haw. Scale bars = 1 cm. Artist Susan Laurie-Bourque. Previously appeared in *Annals of the Missouri Botanical Garden* 85: 478 (1998). Reprinted with permission of the journal ©.

a significant problem. This hybrid is responsible for three of the best reddish-flowered hawthorns: 'Paul's Scarlet', 'Punicea', and 'Rubra Plena'.

'Paul's Scarlet' (synonyms *C. laevigata* 'Coccinea Flore Pleno' W. Paul, *C. monogyna* var. *paulii* Rehder): The true form is a double-flowered crimson or scarlet and is in the trade in western Europe but not known in North America. It originated as a sport of 'Rubra Plena' to which it is apparently constantly reverting back. True 'Paul's Scarlet' is said to be crimson, in spite of its name. Forms more truly scarlet in color are also known and may be mutants or perhaps variants caused by soil conditions. This is one of the most spectacular cultivated hawthorns. Plates 34, 35.

'Punicea': This fine, single, red-flowered form is similar in color to 'Paul's Scarlet'. I have only seen it twice, once at the Royal Botanic Gardens, Kew, the other time at Royal Botanic Gardens, Hamilton, Ontario, but both trees appear to have gone by 2000. Plate 36.

'Punicea Plena': This name may not be correct for this particularly deep-colored double-flowered form but it fits. A plant may be seen at the Saltwells Nature Reserve, West Midlands, United Kingdom.

'Rubra Plena' (synonym *C. ×media* 'Rosea Plena'): The double flowers are carmine-pink. Grown well, it is a very desirable plant. It is commonly grown but usually sold in North America as 'Paul's Scarlet'. Plate 37.

Crataegus mexicana Moçiño & Sessé
tejocote
synonym *C. stipulosa* (HBK) Steudel
Plates 38, 39, 40

Crataegus mexicana is a large bush or small tree to 7 m, with thorns that are usually numerous, medium-sized, and straight to more or less recurved. The leaves are approximately elliptic, not lobed, and medium-sized to small. The medium-sized flowers are more or less numerous in an inflorescence, and are followed by generally large, subglobose, thick-stalked usually yellow to orange fruit containing 4–5 nutlets. The undersides of the young leaves and inflorescence branches are densely hairy.

This species is widespread in the mountains of Mexico from the central highlands near Mexico City down to Chiapas. It also extends as a wild plant into Guatemala and it has been introduced into the Andes of Peru and Ecuador where it is usually called *Crataegus stipulosa*. It is hardy in zones 9–11, and northwest European introductions were periodically wiped out by cold winters. *Crataegus mexicana* could be successfully grown in southern California, the American Gulf Coast, and the Mediterranean littoral. A form grown in England as *C. stipulacea* Loddiges is reckoned to be hardier (Hillier 1981).

Crataegus mexicana is known as tejocote in Mexico, a name also somewhat indiscriminately given to other Mexican hawthorns. It is an important food crop in the highlands of the southern half of Mexico and in Central America. Selected forms are left growing in fields and gardens, but at other times obviously clonal stock is cultivated in proper orchards (Plate 40). The popularity of the fruit is probably on the decrease, however, as more people have access to apples.

This species has often been called *Crataegus pubescens* (HBK) Steudel in the literature, but this name is inadmissible, being a later homonym of *C. pubescens* (K. Presl) K. Presl, a Sicilian species. Furthermore, *C. pubescens* (HBK) Steudel is correctly referred to *C. gracilior* J. B. Phipps, a member of the *crus-galli* group. Interestingly, Eggleston (1909) had recognized that *C. pubescens* (HBK) Steudel

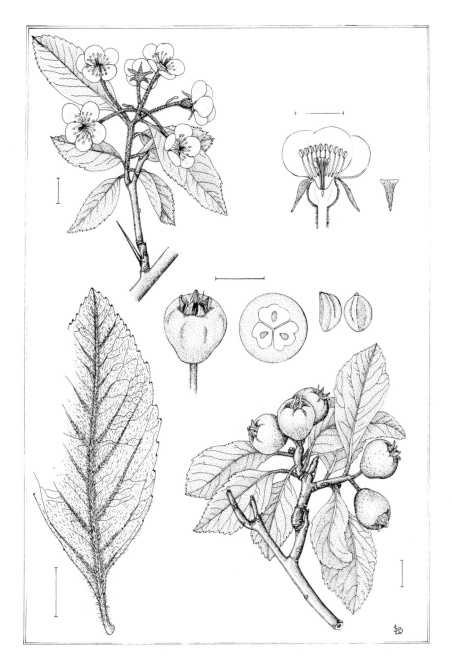

Figure 7.6. *Crataegus mexicana*, tejocote. Scale bars = 1 cm. Artist Susan Laurie-Bourque. Previously appeared in *SIDA, Botanical Miscellany* 15: 29 (1997). Reprinted with permission of the Botanical Research Institute of Texas ©.

was different from *C. mexicana* as early as the beginning of the 20th century, and it is curious that this was overlooked for so long.

As an ornamental, this species should make a handsome small tree in selected forms. The large yellow or orange fruit is nearly unique in *Crataegus* and can be very handsome as well as being edible.

Crataegus mollis (Torrey and A. Gray) Scheele, s.l.
    downy hawthorn
    including *C. arkansana* Sargent, *C. texana* Buckley

Crataegus mollis is a large shrub or small tree 5–10(–14) m tall of varying thorniness. The thorns are stout, medium length, somewhat recurved, and generally brownish at 2 years. The leaves are medium-sized to large, broad-elliptic to ovate, and variously lobed, from very deeply (var. *incisa*, var. *sera*) to very shallowly (many *texana* and *arkansana* biotypes). They are densely hairy when young, the hairs often persisting to maturity. The tomentose inflorescence bears many medium-sized flowers that are followed by subglobose to somewhat pyriform bright red, often still hairy fruit, usually containing 5 nutlets.

Downy hawthorn is a mostly trans-Appalachian species with a wide range from eastern Texas north to Minnesota and east to Ohio and Alabama. It is, however, rare in the southeastern quarter of this range. It generally grows in open habitats and occurs in zones 5–8. The U.S. National Champion in 1998 was 15.8 m tall when last measured in 1972 in Grosse Ile, Michigan.

Crataegus mollis can make a handsome landscape specimen when well-grown, and searching for superior forms in the wild is recommended. It is the state flower of Missouri, where it is quite common. The downy nature of the plant, best observed near flowering time, is both distinctive and attractive; the tree is floriferous and the red fruit can be plentiful.

Crataegus submollis Sargent (Figure 7.7) of the northeastern United States and adjacent Canada is related to *C. mollis* but can be distinguished from the latter by its wholly allopatric distribution, 10 stamens, less treelike habit, and greater thorniness, among other traits. For a particularly hardy, large bush feature, with well-grown, strikingly large, cherry-like abundant fruit and the ability to generate autumnal color in the foliage, *C. submollis* should be considered in the Great Lakes area, Quebec, and New England.

Another relative is *Crataegus viburnifolia* Sargent, only known from near Houston, Texas. It is, in effect, a bright yellow-fruited *C. texana*. The species is perhaps hardy to zone 7 and would make a fine ornamental for mild winter areas.

Figure 7.7. *Crataegus submollis*. The typically huge crop of this species is comprised of almost cherry-sized brilliant scarlet fruit. Bruce Peninsula, southern Ontario, Canada. (photo J. B. Phipps)

Crataegus monogyna Jacquin
one-seeded hawthorn
Plates 41, 42, 43

Crataegus monogyna is a large bush or small tree capable of reaching more than 10 m tall. It is characterized by small, deeply dissected, nearly glabrous (except in southern Europe and North Africa) leaves with veins to sinuses. Thorns are indeterminate, and the usually glabrous inflorescences bear small flowers followed by dull red, smallish, ellipsoid to globose fruit with a single nutlet. One-seeded hawthorn is found throughout Europe (except the north) and Russia and extends into northern Africa and western Asia. It has been introduced into the United States, Canada, and various temperate countries of the Southern Hemisphere. It grows best in sunny, open places and dislikes heavy shade. In cultivation, it is best in zones 5–7 and is not really suited to hot dry summers without a source of groundwater.

The nearest relatives among common hawthorns are *Crataegus meyeri*, *C. pseudo-heterophylla*, *C. rhipidophylla*, and *C. songarica*, none of which is treated in this book. Hybrids with *C. laevigata* are treated under *C. ×media*, which see. The common name English hawthorn is not used here because *C. monogyna* ranges over a region 30–40 times the area of England.

Crataegus monogyna has given rise to a number of interesting cultivars (see key). Well-grown, the best of these and the wild type are excellent ornamentals for landscape purposes. This hawthorn is the main component of hawthorn hedges in the northern half of Europe.

KEY TO CULTIVARS OF *C. monogyna*

1. Flowering twice, in December and again in May . . . . 'Biflora'
1. Flowering once, in May
  2. Stems twisted . . . . 'Flexuosa'
  2. Stems not twisted
    3. Branches pendulous . . . . 'Pendula'
    3. Branches not pendulous
      4. Flowers pink . . . . 'Rosea'
      4. Flowers not pink
        5. Flowers red
          6. Flowers deep red . . . . 'Punicea'
          6. Flowers bright crimson, center white . . 'Crimson Cloud'
        5. Flowers white or bicolored
          7. Flowers bicolored (margins pink-red,
            center white) . . . . 'Bicolor'
          7. Flowers white
            8. Leaves variegated . . . . 'Variegata'
            8. Leaves green
              9. Branches erect . . . . 'Stricta'
              9. Branches spreading
                10. Fruit yellow . . . . 'Aurea'
                10. Fruit red . . . . all other cultivars and
                             wild-type *C. monogyna*

Crataegus okanaganensis J. B. Phipps & O'Kennon
Okanagan hawthorn
Plate 44

Crataegus okanaganensis is a large shrub to 8 m tall with stout, straight, and short-ish thorns. The leaves are medium-sized, more or less ovate or ovate-rhombic to elliptic-oblong, broader forms sharply lobed, narrower forms barely lobed. Inflo-rescences have numerous small flowers. The subglobose to ellipsoid or flask-shaped fruit is brilliant red about the last week of August, turning deep purple at full maturity. The long pointed calyx lobes of the fruit contain 2–4 nutlets and are conspicuous.

Okanagan hawthorn is the most abundant of a group of mainly recently dis-covered species (Phipps and O'Kennon 1998, 2002) that range from a little west of the Okanagan of British Columbia and Washington to northwest Montana. All the hawthorns of this region occur in valleys where their habitat may be natural hedges, ditches, oxbow margins, and other locally damp places.

This is a fine hawthorn with excellent potential as an ornamental. It is most striking in the latter parts of August, the abundant, brilliant red fruit contrasting with bright green foliage and creating a hollylike effect. In late September, autumn foliage colors are dominated by bronzy copper hues and are also attractive.

The related *Crataegus enderbyensis* J. B. Phipps & O'Kennon, with convex, leath-ery leaves, is also highly recommended as an ornamental.

Crataegus okennonii J. B. Phipps
O'Kennon hawthorn
Plates 26, 45

Crataegus okennonii, a segregate from *C. douglasii*, is perfectly easy to distinguish when in good condition. The former is generally taller, more erect, and treelike in its growth, with shorter thorns. The leaf shape differs subtly from Douglas haw-thorn, the flowers are markedly larger, and the fruit ripens differently, through redder-brown shades, and is much less bloomy. O'Kennon hawthorn ranges widely through the valleys of the Pacific Northwest and southern British Columbia but does not turn up east of the Rocky Mountains as *Crataegus douglasii* does. The two occur in similar habitats.

Well-grown, *Crataegus okennonii* should be a good ornamental with nice plant habit, though there is as yet no known horticultural experience with trees of repro-

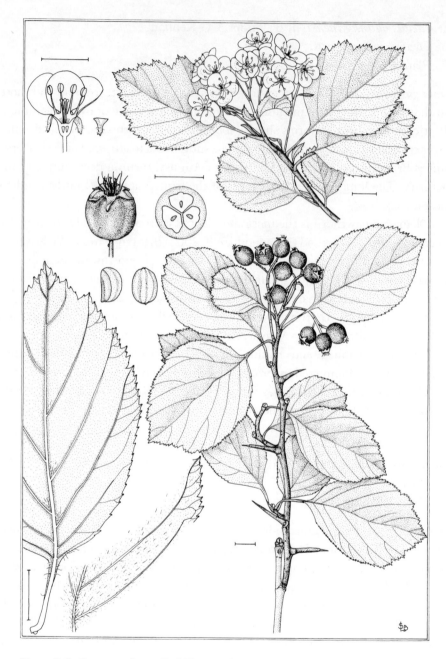

Figure 7.8. *Crataegus okennonii*, O'Kennon hawthorn. Scale bars = 1 cm. Artist Susan Laurie-Bourque. Previously appeared in *SIDA* 18: 173 (1998). Reprinted with permission of the Botanical Research Institute of Texas ©.

ductive age. In fall the foliage of some specimens has been noted to turn to a brilliant cerise color. This hawthorn is generally ornamentally superior to *C. douglasii*. The color changes of the fruit during ripening, which pass from a fairly bright red (Plate 45) through reddish brown (chestnut) to dull purple and nearly black, are very interesting. In spring 2002 co-author Bob O'Kennon and I estimated a certainly record height of 15 m for this species, south of Armstrong, British Columbia. This could be considered a superior ornamental where well suited.

Crataegus orientalis M. Bieberstein

oriental hawthorn
synonyms *C. pubescens* (K. Presl) K. Presl, *C. laciniata* subsp. *pojarkovae* (Kossych) Franco
Plate 46

Crataegus orientalis belongs to the same group of hawthorns as *C. azarolus*, that is, small bushes to large trees, with indeterminate thorns and deeply lobed, small, very hairy leaves with veins to the sinuses. The orange to red orbicular fruit has 2–5 pyrenes. Oriental hawthorn is widespread around the Mediterranean from Morocco and Spain extending east through Turkey to Iran. Like all members of this subgroup, it is not very hardy, thriving best in zones (6?) 7–10 in regions of hot dry summers. Its natural habitat is maquis or open woodland. *Crataegus orientalis* is one of the most beautiful cultivated hawthorns as the coral-red fruit on the Edinburgh specimens show. It has been wrongly referred to *C. laciniata* Ucria in the literature.

A plant called *Crataegus schraderiana* Ledebour (Plate 47) in botanic gardens is also apparently a form of *C. orientalis*. Its beautiful burgundy fruit is equally spectacular.

Crataegus pentagyna Waldstein & Kitaibel ex Willdenow

small-flowered black hawthorn
synonym *C. pseudomelanocarpa* Pojarkova
Plate 48

Crataegus pentagyna is a small to large shrub to small tree with indeterminate thorns. The small, deeply lobed leaves have veins to the sinuses. The very small, numerous flowers are followed by subglobose black fruits with 5 nutlets. Small-flowered black hawthorn is a species of the Balkans extending along both sides of the Black Sea to northern Iran and Turkmenistan. It occurs in scrubby places and open woodland. It is hardy in zones 6–9. Forms seen in botanic gardens have pretty, erect black fruit contrasting effectively with yellowish autumn foliage. A wild form from Hungary had very beautiful purple fruit. This species probably performs best in full sun with adequate moisture.

Crataegus phaenopyrum (Linnaeus f.) Medikus
    Washington thorn
    Plate 49

Crataegus phaenopyrum is usually grown as a free-standing tree to 10 m tall but may be smaller in nature. It has fine, determinate thorns and glossy, somewhat deltate, lobed leaves with veins to the sinuses. The small, plentiful flowers in a domed inflorescence are the latest of any hawthorn and are followed by very small, shiny, orange to vermillion subglobose fruit with 3–4 nutlets.

Washington thorn occurs naturally in the southern half of the eastern United States, apparently being most plentiful in North Carolina and Missouri. It is found in zones 7–9 but is hardy to zone 5. The origin of the vernacular name is unknown to me but presumably is a reference to Washington, D.C. The U.S. National Champion for 1999 is from Abingdon, Virginia, and stood 11 m high in 1989.

In North America Washington thorn is one of the most widely cultivated hawthorns. It has many virtues: outstanding habit; healthy, glossy leaves that normally resist rust; brilliant bronze-orange fall foliage color; and extremely attractive small, shiny, beadlike vermilion fruit. It is easy to cultivate as far north as zone 5 (I have several specimens in my garden) if the conditions are not too dry. Several cultivars exist, manifesting relatively small differences in habit and fruit size (for example, 'Vaughan').

Crataegus phippsii O'Kennon
    Phipps hawthorn
    Plate 50

Crataegus phippsii is a large shrub or small tree to 6–7 m tall with stout, medium-long thorns. The leaves are medium-sized, more or less broad-elliptic to elliptic-ovate, with shallow rounded lobes. The inflorescence bears smallish flowers followed by small, subglobose fruit that is red in August turning black-purple at full maturity; each fruit contains about 3 nutlets. The young parts are softly hairy.

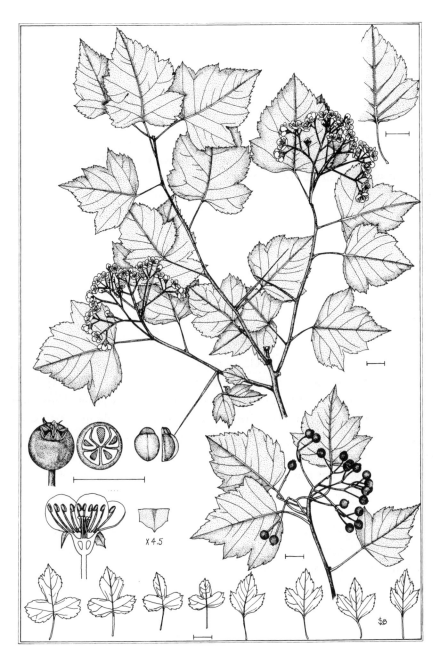

Figure 7.9. *Crataegus phaenopyrum*, Washington thorn. Scale bars = 1 cm. Artist Susan Laurie-Bourque. Previously appeared in *Annals of the Missouri Botanical Garden* 85: 482 (1998). Reprinted with permission of the journal ©.

Phipps hawthorn is a recently discovered species with a wide range from the Okanagan of British Columbia and Washington to near Bozeman, Montana. Like all hawthorns of this area, it is a plant of valleys where it occurs along ditches, draws, creeksides, and natural hedges in the higher rainfall part of the region. In nature it is hardy in zones 5–6.

This hawthorn is particularly attractive to our perhaps biased minds. The somewhat bluish foliage with soft white hair shown on the underside in wind and its particular shape are reminiscent of *Sorbus aria*, a reminder made stronger by the usually substantial clusters of fruit and somewhat treelike habit, which last could easily be encouraged by appropriate pruning in cultivation. In fall the foliage turns attractive shades of dull purple, pure yellow, and orange, an attractive foil for the fruit which ripens to deep purple but which is deep red at the beginning of September.

Crataegus pinnatifida var. major N. E. Brown
sha zhan
Plate 51

Crataegus pinnatifida var. *major* is a large bush or small tree to 6 m tall. The generally thornless twigs bear large, coriaceous, deeply lobed leaves with veins to the sinuses. The medium-sized flowers are borne in large inflorescences. The strikingly handsome subglobose to pyriform fruit is deep red, marked by many conspicuous lenticels, and contains 3–5 nutlets. This hawthorn is restricted to the northern part of eastern China where it grows wild in scrubby places on hillsides. Additionally, it is extensively cultivated for fruit, which is used fresh or in conserves and pies. A valuable nutletless variety has been developed for this purpose. This species is also extensively used in Chinese medicine (see chapter 3). *Crataegus pinnatifida* var. *major* is hardy in zones 5–7. It is a handsome plant when well-grown, with its shiny mid-green leaves and large scarlet fruit, indeed one of the best in *Crataegus*. Other varieties are inferior horticultural subjects.

Crataegus hupehensis Sargent is a similar species with more shallowly lobed leaves.

Crataegus pruinosa (H. L. Wendland) K. Koch, s.l.

frosted hawthorn

including *C. rugosa* Ashe, *C. cognata* Sargent, *C. formosa* Sargent

Plates 52, 53

Crataegus pruinosa is a bush to small tree to 7 m, with very thorny branches. The thorns are medium long, usually straight to slightly recurved, and more or less blackish at 2 years. The leaves are medium-sized; approximately deltate-ovate, ovate, or narrow-ovate; more or less shallowly but sharply lobed; quite glabrous, often bluish; and more or less coriaceous at maturity. The inflorescence bears several medium-sized to very large flowers, followed by subglobose, mauve and green to crimson fruit frequently with abundant pruinosity. There are 3–5 nutlets per fruit and the elevated calyx is distinctive.

In the broad sense, *Crataegus pruinosa* is widely distributed in the eastern half of the United States north to extreme southern Canada and south nearly to the Gulf Coast. In the north it is a scrubby bush of high-light areas, but southward it becomes a small tree of forest understory. The species is hardy in zones 5–8. The U.S. National Champion is from Shenandoah County, Virginia, and was 9.7 m tall in 1991.

As an ornamental, well-grown frosted hawthorn holds promise. It is one of the relatively few eastern North American hawthorns to color well in fall, manifesting a mixture of bright and softer tones in yellows, reds, and oranges. Its main effect at flowering, like that of all hawthorns, is spectacular. The fruit can also be very beautiful and is basically reddish overlaid by pruinosity, often giving a mauve or pink effect; if the pruinosity is abraded, then the fruit may be bright red. It tends to color late and is still often greenish in September. Keeping the foliage in good condition in summer might be a problem due to insects, rust, and dry periods. Northern types tend to sucker, however. Southern examples should be treated as small trees and irrigated well in summer dry periods; while less spectacular in fruit and fall foliage than their northern counterparts, southern types have significant landscape potential.

Crataegus pulcherrima Ashe

beautiful hawthorn

Crataegus pulcherrima is the type of series *Pulcherrimae*, a group of southern U.S. hawthorns that have hardly appeared in the floristic literature since their debut in 1903. The taxonomy of the perhaps four to eight species is still poorly understood so the species are being treated here collectively.

Series *Pulcherrimae* are shrubs to small trees to 8 m tall possessing most of the characteristics of *Crataegus intricata* except that the plants are generally bigger, the leaves far more variable in shape (unlobed, mendosa type; deeply and sharply lobed, incilis type; rounded lobes, robur or illustris type; around the central tendency, pulcherrima type), the trunk bark deeply corrugated, and stamens always 20.

The beautiful hawthorns occur along the American Gulf Coast from extreme southeast Texas to the Florida panhandle, thence east to the Atlantic and extending 160–320 kilometers northward. They are found in open woodland, cutover woodland, and forest edges. The beautiful hawthorns warrant serious attention as landscape subjects for their attractively varying foliage, good plant habit (trees or strong shrubs), and yellow to red fruit. They are probably hardy to zone 6 but are virtually never cultivated.

Crataegus punctata Jacquin
white haw
Plates 54, 55

Crataegus punctata is a bush or small tree to 7 m tall. It is very thorny with medium-long, more or less slender, often recurved, gray thorns at 2 years old. The branches have ashy gray bark. The leaves are 1.5–2 times as long as broad, tapered into a short petiole, and unlobed or with extremely shallow lobes. The flowers occur mid-season and are medium-sized and fairly numerous in the inflorescence. The medium-sized to large subglobose fruits are generally burgundy, scarlet, or yellow at maturity and contain 3–5 nutlets. White haw is widespread in the northeastern quarter of the United States and adjacent Canada and is found in brushy places, unkempt pastures, fence lines, and woodland margins. It thrives in zones 5–6. The U.S. National Champion in 1998 was 11.6 m tall in 1979 and came from Canaan Valley Park, West Virginia.

Well-grown, *Crataegus punctata* can make an architectural small tree for the home landscape with its tiers of branches particularly conspicuous in winter and at flowering. The name white haw is an excellent vernacular and refers to the plant's very pale bark, especially conspicuous in the natural landscape in early spring (Plate 55). The species is greatly superior as an ornamental to the closely related *C. collina* of the southeastern United States and offers fine plant habit and attractive flowers and fruit (in a wide color range) though little autumn color.

Crataegus rivularis Nuttall ex Torrey & A. Gray
river hawthorn
Plate 56

Crataegus rivularis is a large shrub or small tree to 7 m with more or less straight, fine, short thorns. The bark on 2- to 5-cm thick branches is smooth and copper-colored, with large horizontal lenticels. The leaves are elliptic and more or less unlobed, with fairly sharp marginal teeth. The fairly large, early flowers are followed by striking, burgundy turning black, subglobose fruit with 3–5 nutlets. River hawthorn is a fairly common hawthorn in the northwestern U.S. intermontane zone where it occurs along ditches, creeks, and rivers, sometimes in tremendous numbers. Its natural occurrence is in zones 5–6. This species, when well grown, should be an attractive three-season ornamental, the fruit putting on a particularly fine show where well suited.

Crataegus saligna Greene
willow hawthorn
synonym *C. douglasii* var. *duchesnensis* S. L. Welch

Crataegus saligna is a tall slender, at least until maturity, willowy bush or small tree to 5 m. The bark of the trunk is smooth and copper-colored with cherrylike horizontal lenticels. The fine thorns are usually 2–4 cm long and are more or less straight. The leaves are more or less elliptic, not lobed, with crenate margins, and the small flowers are followed by small purple subglobose fruit that turns black and has 3–5 nutlets. Willow hawthorn is a rather rare plant of creeksides and draws in western Colorado and northeastern Utah. It is probably hardy to zone 4. As an ornamental, it should be of interest for its beautiful, spectacular bark (Figure 7.10); smart green foliage; and interesting, somewhat willowy habit. It is seldom cultivated outside botanical gardens and arboreta.

Crataegus sanguinea Pallas
Siberian hawthorn

Crataegus sanguinea is a scrubby bush with determinate, straight, dark thorns of the typical Asiatic kind, 1–2 cm long. The ovate leaves are fairly shallowly lobed without veins to the sinuses. The young parts of the plant are thickly hairy. The fruit is blood-red usually (occasionally orange-red) and has 3–4 nutlets. This species occurs practically throughout southern Siberia and ranges south into Mongo-

Figure 7.10. *Crataegus saligna*, willow hawthorn. Smooth copper-colored bark with horizontal lenticels. Utah, United States. (photo J. B. Phipps)

lia and extreme north China. It reaches 65° north latitude in parts of Siberia and must be incredibly hardy. Pojarkova (1939) recorded its use as a hedge plant.

Crataegus dahurica Koehne ex C. K. Schneider and *C. maximowiczii* C. K. Schneider are related species of northeastern Asia.

As an ornamental *Crataegus sanguinea* would not be among the top 10 hawthorns, but well-grown it is surely valuable for colder climes; however *C. dahurica* is a much smarter plant for such situations.

Crataegus scabrifolia (Franchet) Rehder

Crataegus scabrifolia is usually an unarmed large bush or small tree to 12 m tall in nature. The leaves are elliptic, lobeless, tooth-margined, and more or less glossy.

Large inflorescences bear small flowers. The usually red or more rarely yellow large subglobose fruit is 15–25 mm in diameter and has 5 nutlets. This species is found in the Chinese provinces of Sichuan and Yunnan in open scrub and mixed forest mainly from 1520 to 2400 m. The edible fruit is sold in local markets. The dark glossy leaves, abundant inflorescences, and striking fruit could make *C. scabrifolia* an interesting ornamental in warm, high-rainfall areas, but it is apparently not cultivated outside China.

Crataegus spathulata Michaux
littlehip hawthorn
Plates 9, 57

Crataegus spathulata is generally a medium-sized to large shrub or small tree with trunk bark that exfoliates to leave a smooth surface. The determinate thorns are short or absent, and the small leaves spathulate to deeply lobed with crenate margins. The compact inflorescences have small flowers and the tiny, subglobose fruit are orange to reddish with 3–5 nutlets. Littlehip hawthorn is found throughout the southeastern United States in scrubby places in zones 7–9 and is probably hardy to zone 6. The U.S. National Champion for 1999 is from Hopeville, Georgia, and stood 10.6 m high in 1997.

Though little used as an ornamental, *Crataegus spathulata* has great potential. Some forms are prettily somewhat compact with rather layered branching and bluish mature foliage. Others are more treelike. The exfoliating trunk bark, very similar to that of *C. marshallii*, has great ornamental merit. The flowers are very pretty and the small fruit can be very attractive in good conditions. The vernacular name is silly as this plant doesn't possess hips.

Crataegus succulenta Schrader ex Link
succulent hawthorn
including *C. macracantha* Loddiges ex Loudon, *C. occidentalis* Britton,
C. pertomentosa Ashe
Plates 58, 59, 60

Crataegus succulenta is often a suckering shrub in the eastern United States and southern Canada, sometimes reaching 5 m high, whereas in the Great Plains and western mountains it is generally a multistemmed shrub of up to 3–4 m. It is very thorny, with stout, recurved thorns of medium length in the West, but sometimes

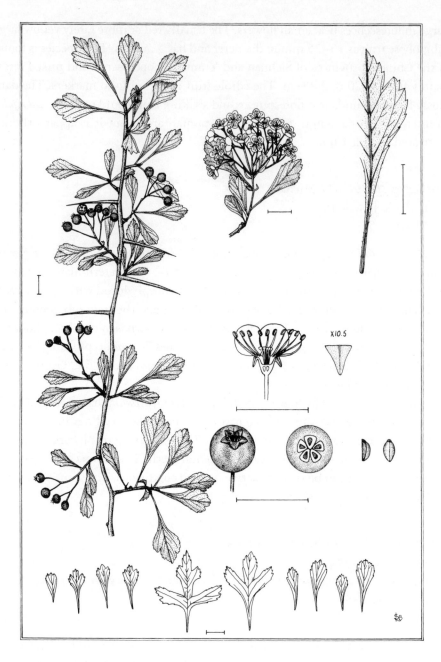

Figure 7.11. *Crataegus spathulata*, littlehip hawthorn. Scale bars = 1 cm. Artist Susan Laurie-Bourque. Previously appeared in *Annals of the Missouri Botanical Garden* 85: 485 (1998). Reprinted with permission of the journal ©.

reaching immense size in the East (11.5 cm in one case). The 2-year-old twigs and thorns are deep purple-brown. The leaves are generally broad-elliptic to elliptic-ovate and generally shallowly lobed. They are often scabrous above when young with variable persistence and glabrous below, except in the case of var. *pertomentosa*, which is densely tomentose. The species flowers in late midseason in the East, but is fairly early in the West. The fruit, which ripens from salmon-orange to bright crimson in the West and from green to deep red in the East, is very juicy at maturity except under dry conditions and contains 2–3 nutlets.

Succulent hawthorn is the most widely ranging hawthorn in North America, occurring in the southern parts of all the Canadian provinces except Newfoundland and in the United States in all the intermontane and Rocky Mountain states as far south as New Mexico and Arizona, the northern Great Plains south to Kansas and Missouri, eastwards from there to the Atlantic as well as south in the Appalachians to North Carolina and Tennessee. It occurs in a variety of brushy habitats.

Crataegus occidentalis is the midwest, Great Plains, and mountain form, with 10 white anthers. *Crataegus macracantha* is a northern and eastern form with 10 pink anthers and generally large thorns. *Crataegus succulenta*, the type form, is eastern and Appalachian and has 20 small, usually red anthers. *Crataegus pertomentosa* represents the western edge of the range of *C. macracantha* and is extremely hairy. Still more variation exists within the main forms than noted above.

Crataegus succulenta is not generally recognized as a superior ornamental and is perhaps best valued for wildlife values and erosion control rather than landscaping. Cultivated plants in Mara and Castlegar, British Columbia, struck me as attractive, densely twigged and foliaged bushes with their apricot-colored fruit in August. Perhaps ancillary irrigation lifted them from their more dowdy congeners. Later, the fruit of these turns a brilliant scarlet. Also the foliage of *C. occidentalis* turns a fine bronzy color in fall. In Ljubljana, capital of Slovenia, I saw one of the most beautiful cultivated hawthorns I have ever come across (Plate 60), outside the Illyria Hotel; it appeared to be this species. These examples emphasize the need to search for superior forms among the more ordinary hawthorns and to cultivate them carefully.

Crataegus tanacetifolia (Poiret) Persoon
tansy hawthorn

Crataegus tanacetifolia belongs to a small group of hawthorns with veins to the sinuses related to the *orientalis-azarolus* group but differentiated from them by the number of pyrenes (4–5) and by the frequent presence on the fruit itself of little

bracts. The leaves are small, deeply lobed, and hairy. The fruit is yellow. The tree
may reach 9 m in height. Tansy hawthorn is practically restricted to Turkey where
it is widespread and in nature occurs in scrubby places and open woodland. It is
hardy in zones 6–10. This hawthorn will make a very attractive tree in regions to
which it is adapted. Where possible, select for forms with superior fruit color.

Crataegus tracyi Ashe ex Eggleston
   Tracy hawthorn
   Plate 61

Crataegus tracyi is a dense thorny bush or small tree to 5 m with narrow obovate,
unlobed, sharp-toothed, and glossy leaves. The inflorescences have several medium-
sized flowers, which are followed by crimson, subglobose, hairy fruit containing
3–5 nutlets. Leaves, young shoots, and flower stalks are also very hairy. This species
has a substantial distribution in central and western Texas as well as the mountains
of Coahuila and Nuevo León in Mexico. Forms from the Davis Mountains in Texas
are hardy to zone 5. Tracy hawthorn is potentially an important ornamental,
though seldom used as such. Its smart *crus-galli*-like, dark green, glossy leaves turn
a fine burgundy in fall while the red fruit is very attractive and may be abundant.

   The closely related *Crataegus aurescens* J. B. Phipps (Plate 62) from Coahuila and
Nuevo León in Mexico is possibly an even finer ornamental with its yellow fruit that
turns orange. It is probably much less hardy.

Crataegus triflora Chapman
   three-flowered hawthorn
   Plate 63

Crataegus triflora is a multistemmed bush to 4 or 5 m with medium-sized, more or
less slender thorns that are blackish at 2 years old. The leaves are very hairy,
medium to large in size, more or less elliptic to ovate, and unlobed or with a few
shallow lobes. The flowers are generally in few-flowered (not necessarily 3-flow-
ered) inflorescences and are usually rather large (25 mm in diameter) with numerous stamens. The fruit is subglobose, hairy, red with very long, spreading calyx
lobes, and is of medium size. It is usually borne singly and contains 3–5 nutlets.
The species has a scattered distribution from Louisiana to Georgia, north into Tennessee, in zones 7–8. It is found in prairie margins, woodland understory, and
cutovers but is seldom common.

Three-flowered hawthorn is one of the most beautiful and distinctive hawthorns of the southeastern United States and it is amazing that it is not in general
cultivation. The unique multitrunked bush is like *Kolkwitzia* in habit but laxer,
with abundant large flowers the size of a small wild rose; the flowers and handsome red fruit are considerable assets. In spite of the name "triflora," as many as 12
flowers per inflorescence can occasionally be encountered. The plant probably needs
protection from drought and may perform best in light shade.

Crataegus uniflora Münchhausen
one-flowered hawthorn
Plate 64

Crataegus uniflora is usually a small bush around 1 m tall, occasionally considerably
bigger. It is very thorny with short fine thorns. The leaves are very small and more
or less elliptic to narrow obovate, without lobes, and with crenate margins. The
inflorescences are 1- to few-flowered with small flowers having unusually long (as
long as petals) pectinate calyx lobes. The fruit is yellowish to ruddy, subglobose,
and hairy with reflexed calyx lobes. Each fruit has 4–5 nutlets.

One-flowered hawthorn has a wide range from Texas to Long Island and inland
to Missouri and Tennessee with an outlier in northeastern Mexico. It generally
occurs in open sandy woodland and scrub. The U.S. National Champion for 1998
was from Gainesville, Florida, and measured 5.5 m tall in 1992; however, most
specimens are usually very much smaller than this.

This hawthorn is usually much too scrappy to be a top-class ornamental, yet it
should be seriously considered for xeriscaping. Fine forms are potentially there for
discovery, for instance, a very dwarf, dense form from Georgia that flowers at 30 cm
in height. The compact nature of this plant emphasizes and concentrates the deep
green of the leaves against which the flowers stand out as little white stars. The
hardiest forms would probably survive in zone 6.

Crataegus ×*vailiae* Britton
Vail's hawthorn
Plate 65

Crataegus ×*vailiae* is a medium-sized thorny shrub with more or less unlobed, somewhat rhombovate small to medium-sized leaves. Inflorescences are fairly few-flowered with conspicuously glandular sepals. The fruit is yellow to orange-red,

medium-sized, subglobose, and often slightly hairy; it contains 3–5 nutlets. Well-grown, this is an attractive, somewhat dense bush with bright green rather glossy and stiff foliage. It is frequently seen in arboreta but is not in commerce to my knowledge. In the wild it has a scattered distribution from Missouri to Virginia where it is a weakly persisting hybrid of *C. uniflora* × (probably) *C. calpodendron*.

Crataegus viridis Linnaeus
green hawthorn
Plate 66

Crataegus viridis is a large shrub or small tree to 10 m or more. The trunk bark is attractively exfoliating, particularly strikingly so in the *glabriuscula* form of Texas to Oklahoma. The twigs usually have medium-long, somewhat fine, often recurved thorns. The leaves are extremely variable in shape for a single species: rhombic and lobed, elliptic to obovate and unlobed, or lanceolate to oblong and unlobed. They are bright green and somewhat shiny when young. Plant parts are usually more or less glabrous. The inflorescence normally has fairly numerous medium-sized flowers, followed by very small red to yellow fruit containing about 3–4 nutlets.

This species ranges widely through the southeastern United States from central Texas and Oklahoma east to the Atlantic and north to Missouri and tidewater Virginia. It is characteristically a species of bottomlands. Selected forms are hardy to zone 5, but this is probably not true for more southern provenances. The U.S. National Champion for 1998 was from Marlinton, West Virginia, and measured 12.2 m tall in 1981.

Green hawthorn is very variable, and ample opportunity exists to make further desirable selections. At present, 'Winter King' is the cultivar of choice. Its bright red fruit is the size of holly berries and is held well into the winter months. It also has reasonable fall color. Fruit retention is, of course, an extremely important ornamental characteristic and if this could be found in more wild populations, or bred into them, then a wide range of color and attractive bark type could be exploited.

Crataegus nitida Hort. is, in examples that I have seen, no more than a variant of *C. viridis*. Authentic *C. nitida* (Engelmann) Sargent, as known from fairly abundant herbarium material of around 100 years ago, seems no longer to exist.

Crataegus wilsonii Sargent
Wilson's hawthorn
Plate 67

Crataegus wilsonii is a large bush or small tree to 7 m tall. The leaves are ovate and shallowly lobed with veins only to the sinuses. They are often attractively rugose at maturity (see Plate 67). The thorns are 1–2 cm long, straight, dark, and determinate. The flowers are small and numerous in the inflorescence, and the fruit is a shiny red, usually ellipsoid but not infrequently, apparently, subglobose. The young plant parts are markedly hairy. Wilson's hawthorn is found in the mountains of southwestern China at 900 to 3000 m in forest margins. It will make an attractive ornamental in areas where there is little summer drought, though it is seldom cultivated outside botanic gardens and arboreta.

Crataegus oresbia W. W. Smith and *C. chungtienensis* W. W. Smith are very similar.

HYBRID CULTIVATED SPECIES

Crataegus ×grignonensis Mouillefert ex Anonymous
Grignon hawthorn
Plate 68

Crataegus ×grignonensis is a small tree to 5 m, with numerous, medium-short, often recurved thorns. The leaves are more or less elliptic and small with shallowly lobed margins. The multiflowered inflorescence bears small to medium-sized flowers followed by glossy, ellipsoid fruit that, during ripening, turns from yellow to a dull, deep, somewhat brownish red. Each fruit contains 1–2 nutlets.

This hawthorn originated in cultivation in Grignon, France, in 1873 as a seedling of *Crataegus mexicana*. The male parent was unknown but was suspected by the raisers to be *C. crus-galli*. Evidence from the nutlets and leaf shape suggests, however, that the pollen parent is *C. monogyna*. Indeed, if *C. ×lavallei* had as pollen parent *C. crus-galli*, as was commonly suggested, surely something different was required for *C. ×grignonensis* in view of the fact that the seed parent, *C. mexicana*, was unequivocally known in both cases. Grignon hawthorn is hardy in zones 6–8.

Although the authority name is usually cited as Mouillefert ex Wien, the description is actually anonymous and Wien (Vienna) is the place of publication. In the circumstances, this species should be considered as not validly described.

Crataegus ×*grignonensis* is a very pretty small tree with neat foliage, compact inflorescences, and very attractive, somewhat unusually colored fruit, a view shared by Wurzell (1992). I highly recommend it as an ornamental, where suited.

Crataegus ×*lavallei* Hèrincq ex Lavallée
Lavallée hawthorn
including *C.* ×*carrieri* Vauvel ex Carrière
Plate 69

Crataegus ×*lavallei* is a small tree to 6 m tall with medium-long, stout, recurved thorns. The leaves are without lobes, more or less elliptic, and very glossy when young but duller later. The flowers are more or less numerous in the inflorescence and late followed by yellowish-red to orange-red, more or less glossy fruit containing 3–4 nutlets.

This hawthorn originated in cultivation in France about 1867 and was described by A. Lavallée in 1880. *Crataegus* ×*carrieri* originated later from the same parental species and is distinguished by a number of minor differences (see Carrière 1883). If distinguished today, this form is best referred to as 'Carrieri'. Both are quite widely cultivated hawthorns performing best in zones 5–7.

The female parent of *Crataegus* ×*lavallei* is *C. mexicana* and the pollen parent was suspected of being *C. crus-galli*, later generally repeated as fact. An unpublished M.Sc. thesis by a former student of mine, Tom Wells, provides a strong argument that *C. calpodendron* was the male parent. In this context it is interesting to note that *C. calpodendron* was in 19th-century France disguised as *Mespilus fontanesiana* in a number of botanic gardens and that, when it was transferred to *Crataegus* as *C. fontanesiana*, it was thought by some botanists to be a synonym of *C. crus-galli*.

Well-grown, Lavallée hawthorn is a very handsome ornamental with its erect trunk, masses of white flowers, and glossy, bright green becoming dark-green foliage which effects a striking background for the yellow to reddish fruits. Under inferior conditions, its foliage is, however, seriously afflicted by rust and leaf-cutting insects.

Crataegus ×*mordenensis* Boom
Morden hawthorn
Plate 70

Crataegus ×*mordenensis* is a small tree to 7 m. Thorns were not observed. Leaves are small, broad-ovate, and deeply dissected, with veins to both lobes and sinuses. The inflorescence has numerous, medium-sized flowers followed by rich red, glossy ellipsoid fruit containing 2–3 nutlets.

The Morden hawthorn was first raised at the Agriculture Canada Plant Breeding Station in Morden, Manitoba, in 1935. The original form, called 'Toba', has very attractive semi-double blush pink flowers which turn white. It is allegedly a cross of *Crataegus succulenta* s.l. × *C.* ×*media* 'Paul's Scarlet', though in view of the confusion surrounding 'Paul's Scarlet' in North America, the *C.* ×*media* parent may have been 'Rubra Plena'. Seed from 'Toba' produced 'Snowbird', a double white-flowering form.

I have only seen *Crataegus* ×*mordenensis* 'Toba' in British Columbia, where it was a flourishing small tree making a handsome ornamental. The somewhat glossy leaves and fruit created a dramatic effect and on this evidence I can recommend it highly. 'Snowbird' has similar flowers, but they lack the early pinkish cast. Its foliage is much more shallowly lobed and lacks any veins to the sinuses, like its *C. succulenta* grandparent. It also is a good ornamental.

Crataegus ×*persimilis* Sargent
plumleaf hawthorn
C. prunifolia (Poiret) Persoon, illegitimate name
Plate 71

Crataegus ×*persimilis* is a large bush usually less than 5 m tall. It is very thorny with stout, recurved thorns that are blackish and shiny at 2 years old. The broadly elliptical leaves are unlobed and very shiny. The small to medium-sized abundant flowers are followed by scarlet, subglobose fruit containing 2–3 nutlets.

This hybrid probably originated independently both in cultivation and in the wild. (Because it is one of the more frequently offered hawthorns by nurseries and most readers will only ever encounter forms of horticultural origin, I am treating it here with the other hybrid hawthorns.) Parents are *Crataegus crus-galli* s.l. × *C. succulenta* s.l. Wild material has a scattered distribution around the southern Great Lakes. The plant is hardy to zone 5.

Plumleaf hawthorn is one of the most excellent ornamental hawthorns. The dense glossy foliage generates an effect of mass, enlivened by the abundant creamy white flowers or red fruit. In fall the foliage may turn yellow or bronzy-red, either way a striking performance. The plant grows very well in Britain and in zones 5–6 in North America. It can be raised true from seed. The common name is a translation of *Crataegus prunifolia*, which had gained currency before it was discovered to be illegitimate.

CHAPTER 8

Medlars and
Intergeneric Hybrids

*M*espilus differs from *Crataegus* on the basis of large flowers, notched petals, large number of stamens, multiple stems, lack of thorns on mature wood, narrow, lobe-less leaves with camptodromous venation, fruit with numerous stone cells, and erect calyx lobes. A few species of *Crataegus* have one or two of these characteristics, but not most of them. The intergeneric sexual and graft hybrids are placed in this chapter because of their greater superficial similarity to *Mespilus* rather than to *Crataegus*. The medlars as a whole are valuable ornamentals, and *M. germanica* is a minor fruit. The sexual hybrid ×*Crataemespilus* is an excellent ornamental.

Mespilus canescens J. B. Phipps
  Stern's medlar
  Plates 72, 73

Mespilus canescens is a multistemmed shrub to 7 m tall with exfoliating bark. The mature shoots are without thorns. The smallish, elliptic leaves have no lobes and only the smallest of teeth. The elongating inflorescences turn prettily upward at their ends to display the large flowers with the characteristic medlar-notch to the petals. These are followed by small, bright scarlet, somewhat glossy fruit containing 5 nutlets.

This species is one of the rarest wild plants only known from a population of 30 or so in a protected area in Arkansas, where it grows in a heavy alluvial clay in the rice belt that is periodically flooded. Its hardiness range still requires evaluation, but in nature it is found in zone 7.

Stern's medlar is arguably the most exquisite ornamental treated in this book. The exfoliating bark is beautifully marbled in ochre, cream, and olive. The plant

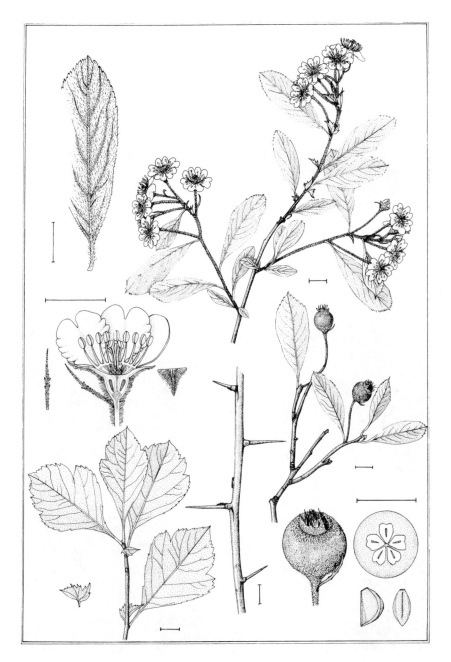

Figure 8.1. *Mespilus canescens*, Stern's medlar. Scale bars = 1 cm. Artist Susan
Laurie-Bourque. Previously appeared in *Systematic Botany* 15: 27 (1990).
Reprinted with permission of the American Society of Plant Taxonomists ©.

Figure 8.2. *Mespilus canescens*, Stern's medlar. The exfoliating bark of this species is beautifully marbled in shades of olive green, cream, and different tones of pale brown. Arkansas, United States. (photo J. B. Phipps)

habit is like that of the beauty bush, *Kolkwitzia*, densely multistemmed and with arching branches. The plant is a fountain of white flowers against somewhat blue-green leaves, and the fruit is a brilliant red color that is rare in hawthorn or medlars. In addition, the fall color consists of attractive tones of pale yellow. This medlar is gradually being introduced into commerce.

Mespilus germanica Linnaeus
common medlar
Plate 74

Mespilus germanica is a stout, often multistemmed, more or less thornless bush 4–6 m tall. The narrow elliptic leaves are medium-sized and without lobes. The large flowers are borne singly at the end of shoots and have numerous stamens and very elongated calyx lobes. The fruit is hawthorn-like in fundamentals, but large and brown with flaring calyx lobes and a wide open hypanthium which exposes the 5 nutlets.

The common medlar is native to the Balkans, Turkey, Caucasia, and northern Iran. It has also been widely cultivated for centuries in Europe in zones 5 and milder. In North America it is scarcely known outside botanic gardens and arboreta.

The wild type has small fruit about 1.5 cm in diameter while cultivars have fruit ranging to (allegedly) 7.5 cm in diameter though 4 cm is more common. Medlar fruit is nearly inedible, due to hardness and high astringency, until it is over-ripe, a condition called "bletted." At such a time it is an interesting minor fruit (see chapter 3) because of its pomological properties and its ornamental ones of flower, fall foliage, and fruit. For fruit, cultivars 'Hollandia', 'Nottingham', and 'Russian' are recommended.

×*Crataemespilus grandiflora* (Smith) E. G. Camus
medlar-hawthorn
synonym *Mespilus grandiflora* Smith
Plate 75

×*Crataemespilus grandiflora* is a densely branched bush to 4–5 m, most closely resembling the common medlar in overall appearance but differing in the somewhat smaller flowers and smaller fruit. I have seen a single specimen at the Royal Botanic Gardens, Kew, and its golden fruit turned burgundy. The plant is reportedly sterile. The medlar-hawthorn originated in cultivation around 1800 (Loudon 1838). Parental species are believed to be *Mespilus germanica* × *Crataegus laevigata*. A similar cross, *M. germanica* × *C. monogyna*, occurring in nature, yielded ×*Crataemespilus gillottii* in France in 1875. The medlar-hawthorn is only occasionally grown as an ornamental, but the Kew specimen has excellent ornamental characteristics culminating in the burgundy ripe fruit set against clear soft yellow fall foliage. Hardiness is probably zones 5–8.

+*Crataegomespilus dardarii* Simon-Louis ex Bellair
Bronvaux medlar

+*Crataegomespilus dardarii* was first written up by Bellair in 1899 and is an example of a "graft hybrid" or chimaera, created by grafting twigs of *Crataegus monogyna* onto stock of *Mespilus germanica*. The chimaera created is an unstable mixture of the two species that leads to considerable variation. Indeed, pure *C. monogyna* or *M. germanica* can readily grow out of the chimaera. Beck provides an excellent colored line illustration of this strange plant in Reichenbach and Reichenbach (1903). Bronvaux medlar has no great beauty, but it does have real interest and could constitute a great talking point for the garden. If you cannot buy one, you can create your own.

APPENDIX *1*

Preparation of Herbarium Specimens

T HE SERIOUS STUDENT of hawthorns who wishes to identify them correctly will come to recognize that carefully collected herbarium specimens are a necessity. Fresh material, collected for the purpose and brought rapidly up to the herbarium or library, is naturally excellent for identification, but it is difficult to remember the fine distinctions between species without building up a reference collection. For me, herbarium specimens are axiomatic because I may be encountering large numbers of hawthorn specimens thousands of kilometers from home base. Is information lost in creating a herbarium specimen? Certainly, but this loss need not be serious. The two most important pieces of information on the plant itself that will not be retained on the herbarium specimen are height of plant and color of parts. No problem here; these may be recorded in a notebook.

This appendix looks at the separate elements of preparing specimens, in sequence: the press, collecting specimens, labeling and data recording, drying, mounting, and storage. Various excellent standard works are also available on plant collecting (for example, Foreman and Bridson 1989) and one on hawthorn collecting specifically, the weighty tome by Kruschke (1955).

THE PRESS. A typical plant press consists of two wooden lattice frames held tightly together by straps with nonslip buckles. The dimensions are a little larger than the herbarium sheet on which the specimen will be mounted, typically about 31 × 44 cm. Inside the press is a multilayered repeating sequence of cardboard, flimsies (often newsprint cut to size, but may be any thin absorbent paper), and blotters. The specimen is carefully arranged (for example, leaves spread out to reduce overlap, flowers upwards, thorns bent back forcibly into the plane of the paper) in the flimsy, the flimsy or specimen is labeled, the flimsy closed, and then a blotter and a cardboard is placed on top. The process is repeated for each specimen. Finally the press is *very* tightly strapped up, to be opened again at the next stop. Serious collectors will make at least one duplicate of each collection. The first specimen belongs to the collector, the duplicate would be offered (this is protocol) to a herbarium that makes the determination.

An alternative press used by hawthorn expert Emil Kruschke is shown in his *Hawthorns of Wisconsin* (1955). Such elaborate things are rarely encountered, however, as they are so cumbersome. If you have this publication, still available by mail order, note Kruschke's lab press as well as his field press. In case you wish to laugh, Kruschke's collections were among the best ever made.

THE SPECIMEN. It is to important to minimize the delay between cutting the specimen and pressing it due to potential damage such as severe wilting, breakage, or possible loss of parts. There is also the problem of confusing the collection sites if the specimens from one location are not pressed before proceeding to the next location. Hawthorn flowers are very fragile and hawthorn fruits tend to break off readily, so press immediately! A good specimen will show typical leaves and thorns as well as flowers or fruit. Old, gnarled branches will not press well. If available, select straight, fairly rapidly growing shoots 25–30 cm long and cut them with a sharp knife or pruning shears. If not feasible to press specimens immediately, they may be carried carefully for a while in a large plastic bag. Each collected specimen needs a numbered tag, or a number written on the sheet of the plant press in which it is placed, at the time of collection. This number is for identification and cross-references the recorded data (see below).

REFERENCE DATA. All herbarium specimens collected need to have their collection data cross-referenced into a field notebook at the time of collection. This includes the following pieces of information:

- A UNIQUE NUMBER. This number is entered into the accession book and must also be with the specimen (see above). The number identifies the collection itself and is preceded by the collector's name. In the example *P. G. Smith 1000*, the name of the collector is P. G. Smith, and 1000 represents his one-thousandth collection. All duplicates from the same tree collected on the same day receive the same number.
- DATE. Not only does the date remind you of the circumstances of collection, but it is also essential in later interpretations of flowering sequence. This will assume greater significance with experience.

- LOCATION. This information needs to be precise enough to pinpoint on a map. Detailed directions to a particular tree are usually left with the field notes. Location information should be carefully stratified: country, state or province, county or district, distance and direction from the nearest town or road junction. Roads need to be accurately referenced by number or name. Professional collectors will provide latitude and longitude co-ordinates accurate to the nearest minute. For this, GPS is most helpful. Township, range, and section (in the United States) make a good alternative. If collecting among mountains or along rivers and creeks, these should be named. On private land, the name of the property owner is helpful.
- HABITAT. This information indicates whether a particular species likes dry or wet places, sun or shade, sand or limestone, and so forth. It should be kept brief, generally under 10 words. Under this heading indicate the frequency of the plant.
- OTHER. In this category, record anything else that strikes you as relevant and interesting, perhaps usage, pollinators, or dispersers.
- MISSING DATA. Because you are not making a herbarium specimen of an entire plant, you need to record data that you do not collect, or what will be lost on drying, which for hawthorns is height; bark type; compound thorns, if any, on trunk; if flowers, fresh anther color, petal color if other than white; if fruit, fresh fruit color to a reasonable degree of precision. Of these, the first is mandatory and the last two very important.

DRYING AND SUBSEQUENT CARE. After 12–24 hours, open the press carefully and inspect each specimen. Re-arrange leaves, if necessary, carefully unfold those that became folded (this can be quite time-consuming), and remove grubs, if any (not unlikely). If the collection was made in rain, the blotters will be fairly damp. Exchange them for dry blotters. Finally, dry the contents of the press as fast as feasible, using a field drier, hot sun, or a lab drier set to about 40°C and supplied with forced air to prevent overheating on return to base. Attention to these matters is the difference between poor and excellent specimens, between ease of correct identification and great difficulties with same, and also between your personal satisfaction or dismay.

MOUNTING. Specimens are mounted with glue or tape on 40 × 30 cm, stiff, acid-free herbarium mounting sheets (see Foreman and Bridson 1989). Various herbarium supply companies provide these materials. At the time of mounting a permanent label containing the collection information as outlined above is generated, usually today by computer, to be glued in the bottom right corner of the herbarium sheet.

STORAGE. Professional herbarium collections are stored in steel cabinets of standard size, but the amateur may be satisfied with cardboard boxes, if kept in dry conditions. In all cases specimens should be mounted to avoid damaging loose collections. Steel cabinets are preferred as they are stable, moderately fireproof, and somewhat insect-proof. Herbarium specimens have several problems. They are very fragile and easily damaged by casual movement. They also are very flammable. Furthermore, they may get infested with insects able to survive on organic material containing less than 1 percent water, such as dried specimens. The responsible insects, usually dermestid beetles, may destroy a collection. Insects may be kept at bay by use of permanent fumigants, but few if any are environmentally acceptable today, or by low temperature storage (anything below 14.5°C) which leaves dermestids in a state of permanent dormancy. Freezing (below −5°C) will kill nondormant dermestids. Please note that dermestids have a preference for hawthorns, particularly their flowers.

Checklist of *Crataegus* and *Mespilus* Species

THIS LIST is modified from Phipps et al. (1990) and Christensen (1992) and includes several new species described by O'Kennon and me as well as horticultural hybrids in *Crataegus*, the medlar (*Mespilus*), and intergeneric hybrids. In addition, this list probably excludes species in inadequately studied groups such as series *Lacrimatae* and *Pulcherrimae*, some distinct but very rare or extinct taxa that are probably interserial hybrids, and a few recently described species by other authors which have not yet been evaluated. The few persistent interserial hybrids included are placed where they would key out best.

Crataegus Linnaeus

I.   Series *Tanacetifoliae* K. I. Christensen
          1. *C. tanacetifolia* (Poiret) Persoon
          2. *C. pycnoloba* Boissier & Heldreich
II.   Series *Orientales* (C. K. Schneider) Pojarkova
          3. *C. azarolus* Linnaeus
          4. *C. orientalis* M. Bieberstein
          5. *C. heldreichii* Boissier
III.   Series *Pentagynae* (C. K. Schneider) Rusanov
          6. *C. pentagyna* Waldstein & Kitaibel ex Willdenow
IV.   Series *Crataegus*
          7. *C. dzhairensis* Vassilczenko
          8. *C. meyeri* Pojarkova
          9. *C. kurdistanica* Hadač & Chrtek
          10. *C. laevigata* (Poiret) A.-P. de Candolle

11. *C. caucasica* K. Koch

12. *C. ambigua* Meyer ex Becker

13. *C. sakranensis* Hadač & Chrtek

14. *C. songarica* K. Koch

15. *C. pallasii* Grisebach

16. *C. karaghadensis* Pojarkova

17. *C. heterophylloides* Pojarkova ex K. I. Christensen

18. *C. longipes* Pojarkova

19. *C. microphylla* K. Koch

20. *C. rhipidophylla* Gandoger

21. *C. nevadensis* K. I. Christensen

22. *C. pseudoheterophylla* Pojarkova

23. *C. monogyna* Jacquin

24. *C. sphaenophylla* Pojarkova

25. *C. heterophylla* Flügge

V.   Series *Cuneatae* (Rehder ex C. K. Schneider) Rehder

26. *C. cuneata* Siebold & Zuccarini

27. *C. tangchungchangii* F. P. Metcalf

28. *C. shandongensis* F. Z. Li & W. D. Peng

VI.   Series *Apiifoliae* (Loudon) Rehder

29. *C. marshallii* Eggleston

VII.   Series *Pinnatifidae* (Zabel ex C. K. Schneider) Rehder

30. *C. pinnatifida* Bunge

31. *C. necopinnata* Pojarkova

VIII.   Series *Cordatae* (Beadle ex Eggleston) Rehder

32. *C. phaenopyrum* (Linnaeus f.) Medikus

IX.   Series *Microcarpae* (Loudon) Rehder

33. *C. spathulata* Michaux

X.   Series *Nigrae* (Loudon) Rusanov

34. *C. nigra* Waldstein & Kitaibel

35. *C. jozana* C. K. Schneider

36. *C. chlorosarca* Maximowicz

37. *C. clarkei* Hooker f.

XI.   Series *Sanguineae* (Zabel ex C. K. Schneider) Rehder

38. *C. dahurica* Koehne ex C. K. Schneider

39. *C. sanguinea* Pallas

40. *C. russanovii* Cinovskis

41. *C. maximowiczii* C. K. Schneider

42. *C. kansuensis* E. H. Wilson

43. *C. chungtienensis* W. W. Smith

44. *C. wilsonii* Sargent

45. *C. oresbia* W. W. Smith

46. *C. aurantia* Pojarkova

XII. Series *Macracanthae* (Loudon) Rehder

47. *C. calpodendron* (Ehrhart) Medikus

48. *C. succulenta* Schrader ex Link

49. *C. macracantha* Loddiges ex Loudon

50. *C.* ×*vailiae* Britton

XIII. Series *Brainerdianae* Eggleston ex E. J. Palmer

51. *C. florifera* Sargent

52. *C. coleae* Sargent

53. *C. brainerdii* Sargent

54. *C. scabrida* Sargent

XIV. Series *Douglasianae* (Rehder ex C. K. Schneider) Rehder

55. *C. suksdorfii* (Sargent) Kruschke

56. *C. douglasii* Lindley

57. *C. okennonii* J. B. Phipps

58. *C. castlegarensis* J. B. Phipps & O'Kennon

59. *C. shuswapensis* J. B. Phipps & O'Kennon

XV. Series *Cerrones* J. B. Phipps

60. *C. erythropoda* Ashe

61. *C. rivularis* Nuttall

XVI. Series *Brevispinae* (E. J. Palmer) Rehder

62. *C. saligna* Greene

63. *C. brachyacantha* Sargent & Engelmann

XVII. Series *Purpureofructi* J. B. Phipps & O'Kennon

64. *C. williamsii* Eggleston

65. *C. okanaganensis* J. B. Phipps & O'Kennon

66. *C. enderbyensis* J. B. Phipps & O'Kennon

67. *C. orbicularis* J. B. Phipps & O'Kennon

68. *C. atrovirens* J. B. Phipps & O'Kennon

69. *C. phippsii* O'Kennon

XVIII. Series *Greggianae* J. B. Phipps

70. *C. greggiana* Eggleston

71. *C. serratissima* J. B. Phipps
72. *C. sulfurea* J. B. Phipps
73. *C. grandifolia* J. B. Phipps

XIX.   Series *Baroussaneae* J. B. Phipps
74. *C. baroussana* Eggleston
75. *C. cuprina* J. B. Phipps
76. *C. johnstonii* J. B. Phipps

XX.   Series *Molles* (Sargent ex C. K. Schneider) Rehder
77. *C. mollis* (Torrey & A. Gray) Scheele
78. *C. ×kellogii* Sargent
79. *C. pennsylvanica* Ashe
80. *C. submollis* Sargent

XXI.   Series *Coccineae* (Loudon) Rehder
81. *C. coccinea* Linnaeus
82. *C. pringlei* Sargent
83. *C. holmesiana* Ashe
84. *C. magniflora* Sargent

XXII.   Series *Tenuifoliae* (Sargent ex Eggleston) Rehder
85. *C. macrosperma* Ashe
86. *C. schuettei* Ashe
87. *C. wootoniana* Eggleston
88. *C. flabellata* (Bosc ex Spach) K. Koch

XXIII.   Series *Silvicolae* (Beadle ex Sargent) E. J. Palmer
89. *C. iracunda* Beadle
90. *C. populnea* Ashe
91. *C. beata* Sargent
92. *C. jesupii* Sargent

XXIV.   Series *Pruinosae* Sargent ex Rehder
93. *C. compacta* Sargent
94. *C. gattingeri* Ashe
95. *C. suborbiculata* Sargent
96. *C. pruinosa* (H. L. Wendland) K. Koch
97. *C. dissona* Sargent

XXV.   Series *Dilatatae* Sargent ex Rehder
98. *C. coccinioides* Ashe

XXVI.   Series *Pulcherrimae* (Beadle ex E. J. Palmer) K. R. Robertson
99. *C. mendosa* Beadle

100. *C. pulcherrima* Ashe
101. *C. illustris* Beadle
102. *C. sargentii* Beadle
XXVII.   Series *Intricatae* Sargent ex Rehder
103. *C. intricata* Lange
104. *C. biltmoreana* Beadle
105. *C. nananixonii* J. B. Phipps
106. *C. padifolia* Sargent
XXVIII.   Series *Rotundifoliae* (Eggleston) E. J. Palmer
107. *C. chrysocarpa* Ashe
108. *C. margaretta* Ashe
109. *C. dodgei* Ashe
XXIX.   Series *Lacrimatae* J. B. Phipps
110. *C. lacrimata* Small
111. *C. lepida* Beadle
112. *C. teres* Beadle
XXX.   Series *Flavae* (Loudon) Rehder
113. *C. aprica* Beadle
114. *C. flava* Aiton
XXXI.   Series *Triflorae* (Beadle ex C. K. Schneider) Rehder
115. *C. triflora* Chapman
116. *C. austromontana* Beadle
117. *C. harbisonii* Beadle
118. *C. ashei* Beadle
XXXII.   Series *Parvifoliae* (Loudon) Rehder
119. *C. uniflora* Münchhausen
XXXIII.   Series *Virides* (Beadle ex C. K. Schneider) Rehder
120. *C. viridis* Linnaeus
121. *C. glabriuscula* Sargent
XXXIV.   Series *Aestivales* (Sargent ex C. K. Schneider) Rehder
122. *C. aestivalis* (Walter) Torrey & A. Gray
123. *C. opaca* Hooker & Arnott
124. *C. rufula* Sargent
XXXV.   Series *Crus-galli* (Loudon) Rehder
125. *C. crus-galli* Linnaeus
126. *C. reverchonii* Sargent
127. *C. gracilior* J. B. Phipps

128. *C. engelmanii* Sargent
129. *C. rosei* Eggleston
130. *C. fecunda* Sargent
131. *C. ✕persimilis* Sargent

XXXVI.   Series *Punctatae* (Loudon) Rehder
132. *C. punctata* Jacquin
133. *C. collina* Chapman
134. *C. jonesae* Sargent

XXXVII.   Series *Mexicanae* (Loudon) Rehder
135. *C. mexicana* Moçiño & Sessé

XXXVIII. Series *Madrenses* J. B. Phipps
136. *C. tracyi* Ashe ex Eggleston
137. *C. aurescens* J. B. Phipps

XXXIX.   Series *Hupehenses* J. B. Phipps
138. *C. hupehensis* Sargent
139. *C. shensiensis* Pojarkova

XXXX.   Series *Henryanae* (Sargent) J. B. Phipps
140. *C. scabrifolia* (Franchet) Rehder

Hybrid taxa only known in horticulture
1. *C. ✕lavallei* Hèrincq ex Lavallée
2. *C. ✕grignonensis* Mouillefert ex Anonymous
3. *C. ✕mordenensis* Boom

Mespilus Linnaeus
1. *M. germanica* Linnaeus
2. *M. canescens* J. B. Phipps

✕*Crataemespilus* E. G. Camus
1. ✕*C. grandiflora* (Smith) E. G. Camus

+*Crataegomespilus* Simon-Louis ex Bellair
1. +*C. dardarii* Simon-Louis ex Bellair

Tabular Key to Hawthorns and Medlars

THIS TABULAR KEY to the species treated in this book includes 20 characteristics helpful in identifying hawthorns and 4 of horticultural significance.

KEY

- PRESENCE/ABSENCE: **Y** = yes; **N** = no.
- RANGES: as specified for a particular character. For example, the ranges for "height" are given in meters, so a height of 4–7 would mean 4–7 meters. Another character might indicate a range of 1–5, with 1 being shortest and 5 longest.
- LEAF LENGTH: 1 = <2 cm; 2 = 2–4 cm; 3 = 4–6 cm; 4 = 6–8 cm; 5 = 8–10 cm.
- LEAF BREADTH: 1 = narrowest (more than twice as long as wide); 5 = broadest (approximately as wide as long).
- PETIOLE LENGTH: 1 = shortest (<20% length of blade); 5 = longest (as long as blade).
- HAIRINESS: 0 = no hair; 1 = thinly hairy; 3 = densely hairy
- FLOWER AND FRUIT DIAMETER: 1 = 6–10 mm; 2 = 11–15 mm; 3 = 16–20 mm; 4 = 20–25 mm; 5 = >26 mm.
- COLOR: **y** = yellow; **o** = orange; **v** = vermilion; **r** = red; **cr** = crimson; **b** = burgundy; **bl** = black; **ma** = mauve; **pk** = pink; **w** = white; **br** = brown; **g** = green.
- LANDSCAPE VALUE: 1 = poor; 5 = excellent; – = no record.

Name	Ht. (meters)	Leaves								
		length: 1 (shortest) – 5 (longest)	breadth: 1 (narrowest) – 5 (broadest)	number of veins per side	veins to sinuses: Y/N	veins to leaf margins: Y/N	lobing: 1 (not lobed) – 5 (deepest sinus reaches midvein)	petiole length: 1 (very short) – 5 (long)	hairy on lower surface young: 0 (no hair) – 3 (densely hairy)	hairy on upper surface young: 0 (no hair) – 3 (densely hairy)
ser. *Aestivales*, Mayhaws	5–9	2–4	2–3	4–9	N	Y	1–2	1	0–2	0–1
C. aprica, sunny hawthorn	2–3	2	4–5	3–4	N	Y	1–2	3–4	0	2
C. azarolus, azarole	6–10	2–4	3	5	Y	Y	5	2	0–2	3
C. brachyacantha, blueberry haw	6–12	2–3	2–3	5–6	N	N	1	2	0	1
C. calpodendron, late hawthorn	5–7	3–4	2–4	8	N	Y	2	1–2	3	2
C. chlorosarca	6	3–5	3	6–9	Y,N	Y	3	2–3	2	2
C. chrysocarpa, fireberry hawthorn	2–3.5	2–3	3–4	5–6	N	Y	2–3	3	0–3	2–3
C. coccinea, scarlet hawthorn	7–12	5	3	5–7	N	Y	2–3	3	0	2
C. coccinioides, Kansas hawthorn	4–7	5	3–4	5–7	N	Y	2–3	3	0	0–2
C. crus-galli, s.l., cockspur hawthorn	5–10	2–4	1	4–7	N	N	1	1	0	0
C. cuneata, cuneate hawthorn	2–3	1–3	2–4	5+	Y	Y	1–5	2	1–3	1–3
C. douglasii, Douglas hawthorn	3–8	2–3	2–3	4	N	Y	2	3	0	3
C. harbisonii, Harbison hawthorn	5–8	3	2–3	6–7	N	Y	1–2	2	2	2
C. intricata, intricate hawthorn	1–5	3–4	2–3	2–3	N	Y	2–3	3	0	0
C. lacrimata, weeping hawthorn	5	1	1–2	3–4	N	Y	1	1	0	0
C. laevigata, woodland hawthorn, midland hawthorn	4–8	2–3	4	4?	Y	Y	3	4	0	0
'Aurea'	4–8	2–3	4	4?	Y	Y	3	3	0	0
'François Rigaud'	4–8	2–3	4	4?	Y	Y	3	3	0	0
'Gireoudii'	4–8	2–3	4	4?	Y	Y	3	3	0	0
'Rosea'	4–8	2–3	4	4?	Y	Y	3	3	0	0
C. macrosperma, eastern hawthorn	3–7	2–3	3	4–7	N	Y	3	3	0	2
C. marshallii, parsley haw	4–8	2	4–5	7–8	Y	Y	5	4	1	3
C. ×media	6–10	2–3	3–4	5	Y	Y	4	4	0	0
'Paul's Scarlet'	6–10	2–3	3–4	5	Y	Y	4	4	0	0
'Punicea'	6–10	2–3	3–4	5	Y	Y	4	4	0	0
'Rubra Plena'	6–10	2–3	3–4	5	Y	Y	4	4	0	0
C. mexicana, tejocote	4–7	2–3	1	6–9	N	N	1	1–2	3	3
C. mollis, downy hawthorn	5–10	3–5	4–5	5–7	N	Y	2–3(4)	3–4	3	3
C. monogyna, one-seeded hawthorn	8–12	2–3	3–5	4?	Y	Y	3–5	4	0(3)	0
C. okanaganensis, Okanagan hawthorn	3–6	3	2–3	4–5	N	Y	2	3	0	1–2

	Inflorescences				Fruit							Landscape Value		
number of flowers (typical)	branches hairy: 0 (no hair) – 3 (densely hairy)	flower diameter as open cup: 1 (small) – 5 (large)	number of stamens	color	diameter: 1 (small) – 5 (large)	shape: 1 (subglobose) – 3 (ellipsoid)	hairiness: 0 (no hair) – 3 (densely hairy)	number of nutlets	nutlets with eroded sides: Y/N	autumn color: 1 (poor) – 5 (excellent)	growth form: 1 (poor) – 5 (excellent)	flower color	fruit abundance/color/impact: 1 (poor) – 5 (excellent)
2–4	0	3	20	r–y	3–4	1	0	5	N	–	–	w	4
3–6	2	3	20	or–r	3	1	0	4–5	N	4	3	w	3
5–21	2	1–3	20	y–or	4	1	3	2–3	N	3	3	w	4
15–25	0	1	20	bl	3	1	0	4–5	N	5	4	w	4
12–25	3	2	20	or–r	2	1–3	0	2–3	Y	2	3	w	4
15–25	0	2	20	bl	2	1	0	4–5	Y	3	–	w	3
5–10	1–3	3	10	r	3	1	3	3–4	N	4	3	w	4
8–15	2	3	5–10	r	4	1	0–2	4–5	N	4	3	w	5
5–12	0	4	20	pk–r	4	1	0	5	N	–	3	w	5
8–20	0	2–3	10–20	r,y	3	1–2	0	1–3	N	4	4	w	5
1–15	0–3	2	20	r,y	4	1	0–2	4–5	N	–	–	w	–
10–25	0	2	10	bl	2	3	0	3–4	Y	3	2	w	3
5–12	3	4	20	r	4	1	0	3–5	N	3	3	w	3
3–8	0	3	10	y–r	3	1	0	3–5	N	2	2	w	3
1–2	0	2	20	r–y	2	1	0	3–4	N	2	5	w	3
3–11	0	2–4	20	r	3	1	0	2–3	Y	3	3	w	4
3–11	0	2–4	20	y	3	1	0	2–3	Y	3	3	w	5
3–11	0	2–4	20	y	3	1	0	2–3	Y	3	3	w	5
3–11	0	2–4	20	r	3	1	0	2–3	Y	3	3	w	5
3–11	0	2–4	20	r	3	1	0	2–3	Y	3	3	pk	5
5–12	0	2	5–10	r	3	1	0	3–5	N	2	2	w	3
12–17	3	2–3	20	r	1	3	0	1–2	N	3	4	w	4
15–30	0	2	20	r	3	1	0	2	N	3	4	w	3
15–30	0	2	few	r	3	1	0	2	N	3	4	r	3
15–30	0	2	20	r	3	1	0	2	N	3	4	r	3
15–30	0	2	few	r	3	1	0	2	N	3	4	pk	3
3–12	3	3	20	or–y	5	1	1	4–5	N	–	3	w	5
5–15	3	4	20	r,y	4	1	3	5	N	3	3	w	5
5–15	0(3)	2	20	r	3	1,2	0	1	N	3	4	w	3
10–20	2	2	10	r>pur	3	2,3	1–2	2–4	N,Y	4	3	w	5

Name	Ht. meters	Leaves length: 1 (shortest) – 5 (longest)	breadth: 1 (narrowest) – 5 (broadest)	number of veins per side	veins to sinuses: Y/N	veins to leaf margins: Y/N	lobing: 1 (not lobed) – 5 (deepest sinus reaches midvein)	petiole length: 1 (very short) – 5 (long)	hairy on lower surface young: 0 (no hair) – 3 (densely hairy)	hairy on upper surface young: 0 (no hair) – 3 (densely hairy)
C. okennonii, O'Kennon hawthorn	6–10	2	3	4–5	N	Y	1–2	3	0	2
C. orientalis, Oriental hawthorn	4–6	2–3	3	5–7	Y	Y	5	1	3	3
C. pentagyna, small-flowered black hawthorn	5–8	2	4–5	4–5	Y	Y	4	3	1	2
C. phaenopyrum, Washington thorn	4–10	2–3	4–5	6–7	Y	Y	2–3	5	0	0
C. phippsii, Phipps hawthorn	5–6	3	3	4	N	Y	2	2	2	3
C. pinnatifida var. *major*, sha zhan	4–6	4–5	3	7–10	Y	Y	2–3	3	0	0
C. pruinosa, frosted hawthorn	2–8	2–3	2–5	5–6	N	Y	2–4	4	0	0
C. pulcherrima, beautiful hawthorn	2–7	2–3	1–3	4–11	N	Y	1–3	3–4	0	0
C. punctata, white haw	4–8	2–3	1–2	7–10	N	Y	1–2	2	1	2
C. rivularis, river hawthorn	3–5	2–4	1–2	4–5	N	N	1–2	2	0	2
C. saligna, willow hawthorn	3–5	2–3	1–2	6–9	N	N	1	2	0	2
C. sanguinea	2–4	2–3	3–4	4	Y,N	Y	2	2–3	1	3
C. scabrifolia	6–12	3–4	4–5	8–14	N	N	1	3	0	2
C. spathulata, littlehip hawthorn	3–7	1	1–2	3–4	Y	Y	1–3	1	1	0
C. succulenta, succulent hawthorn	4–7	2–3	3	6–8	N	Y	2–3	2	0–3	0–3
C. tanacetifolia, tansy hawthorn	5–10	2	3	5–6	Y	Y	5	1–2	3	3
C. tracyi, Tracy hawthorn	4–8	4	1–2	6	N	Y	1	1–2	1	3
C. triflora, three-flowered hawthorn	4–5	2–4	2–4	5–7	N	Y	1–2	3	3	3
C. uniflora, one-flowered hawthorn	1–2	1	2	3	N	N	1	1	2	3
C. ×*vailiae*, Vail's hawthorn	2–5	2–3	3	4–5	N	Y	2	3	2	2
C. viridis, green hawthorn	8–15	2–4	1–4	3–5	N	Y	1–3	3–4	0	0
C. wilsonii, Wilson hawthorn	7	2–4	3	4–5	Y,N	Y	2–3(4)	3	3	2
C. ×*grignonensis*, Grignon hawthorn	5–6	2–3	2	5–8	N	Y	2–3	2	3	3
C. ×*lavallei*, Lavallée hawthorn	8	3	1	8–9	N	N	1	1	1	2
C. ×*mordenensis*, Morden hawthorn	7	3	3–4	3–5	Y	Y	4	4	0	0
C. ×*persimilis*, plumleaf hawthorn	5–6	3	2	6–9	N	Y	1	2	0	2
Mespilus canescens, Stern's medlar	5–7	2–3	1	5–7	N	N	1	2	3	2
Mespilus germanica, common medlar	4–6	3–4	1	8–10	N	N	1	1	3	3

	Inflorescences					Fruit					Landscape Value			
number of flowers (typical)	branches hairy: 0 (no hair) – 3 (densely hairy)	flower diameter as open cup: 1 (small) – 5 (large)	number of stamens	color	diameter: 1 (small) – 5 (large)	shape: 1 (subglobose) – 3 (ellipsoid)	hairiness: 0 (no hair) – 3 (densely hairy)	number of nutlets	nutlets with eroded sides: Y/N	autumn color: 1 (poor) – 5 (excellent)	growth form: 1 (poor) – 5 (excellent)	flower color	fruit abundance/color/impact: 1 (poor) – 5 (excellent)
12–20	0	3	10	r–br>pur–bl	2	1,2	0	3–4	Y,N	5	4	w	4
4–18	3	3	20	or,pur	4	1	3	2–5	Y,N	3	4	w	5
20–40	0–3	1	20	bl	2–3	1	0	3–5	N	3	3	w	3
20–30	0	2	20	v	1	1	0	3	N	5	4	w	5
6–12	3	3	10	r>pur	2	1,2	2–3	3	Y,N	4	3	w	4
15–30	3	3–4	20	r	5	1	0	3–5	N	3	3	w	4
5–10	0	3	20	pk/ma/cr	3	1	0	3–5	N	4	3	w	5
5–10	0	2–3	20	r–y	2	1	0	2–5	N	3	3	w	4
10–25	3	3	20	b,r,y	4	1	1	3–5	N	2	4	w	4
6–12	0	3	10	b>bl	3	1	0	3–4	Y	3	3	w	4
12	0	2	20	bl	2	1	0	3–5	Y	3	4	w	4
10–25	0–1	1	20	r	2	1	0	3–4	Y	–	2	w	3
20–30	0	2	20	r,y	5	1	0	5	N	–	–	w	–
20–30	0	1	20	or–r	1	1	0	3–5	N	3	5	w	5
15–30	0–3	2–3	10,20	r	3	1	0–3	2–3	Y	4	4	w	5
2–9	3	3	20	y	4	1	3	4–5	N	3	4	w	4
6–15	3	3	10,20	r	3	1	3	3–5	N	4	3	w	4
2–6	3	2–5	30+	r	3	1	3	4	N	3	4	w	4
1–3	3	1–3	20	y–or	3	1	3	5	N	3	5	w	3
2–8	3	3	20	or	3	1	3	3–5	Y	4	4	w	4
10–20	0	2	20	r–y	1	1	0	3–4	N	4	4	w	5
20–50	3	2	20	r,?b	2	3	0	2–3	Y	–	–	w	–
15–25	3	1	20	r	3	1	0	1–2	N	3	5	w	5
8–15	3	3	20	or–r	3	1	0	3–4	Y	2	5	w	4
20–25	0	2	few	r	3	1	0	2–3	Y	3	4	w–pk	5
15–25	1	2	20	r	3	1	0	2	Y	4	4	w	4
2–6	3	3	20	r	2	1	1	5	N	3	5	w	4
1	3	5	30	br	5	1	3	5	N	3	3	w	4

Conversion Charts

Millimeters (mm)	Inches	Centimeters (cm)	Inches
1	0.04	0.5	0.2
2	0.08	1	0.4
4	0.15	2	0.8
6	0.25	2.5	1.0
10	0.4	3	1.2
12	0.5	4	1.6
15	0.6	5	2.0
16	0.65	6	2.4
25	1.0	7	2.8
		8	3.2
		9	3.6
		10	4.0
		25	10
		30	12
		40	16
		50	20
		60	24
		75	30
		150	60

Meters (m)	Feet	°Celsius	°Fahrenheit
1	3.25	−40	−40
2	6.5	−35	−31
3	9.75	−30	−22
4	13.0	−25	−13
5	16.25	−20	−4
6	19.5	−15	5
7	22.75	−10	14
8	26.0	−5	23
9	29.25	0	32
10	32.5	5	41
11	35.25	10	50
12	39.0	15	59
13	42.25	20	68
15	48.75	25	77
900	2925	30	86
1500	4875	35	95
2400	7800	40	104
3000	9750		

Hectares	Acres
1	2.5
5	12.5
10	25
20	50
50	125
400	1000

Glossary

acute sharp

agamospermy reproduction by seed but without fertilization (see chapter 4)

allopatric growing in a different region; with non-overlapping distribution

anther the pollen-producing part of the stamen

anthesis flowering

anthropogenic human caused

aphyllous referring to an indeterminate thorn before it has begun to elongate, bear leaves, and perhaps branch; at this stage it resembles a determinate thorn

apomixis reproduction without sexual processes (meaning often restricted to agamospermy)

basal of a part nearest the axis

blade (of a leaf) expanded portion

bract a leaflike organ subtending an inflorescence branch

bracteole a stipulelike organ found in the inflorescence

caducous falling early; early deciduous

calyx lobe sepal, one of the parts of the flower

calyx tube in *Crataegus*, the hypanthium

camptodromous having a venation pattern in which the secondary veins fail to go straight to the edge of the leaf

carpel an individual chamber of an ovary

compound (thorn) branched

cordate heart-shaped (referring usually to the shape of a leaf base), as in the "heart" of playing cards

craspedodromous having a venation pattern in which the secondary veins go straight to the edge of the leaf, usually ending in a lobe tip

crenate having teeth with rounded or blunt ends

cuneate wedge-shaped

deltate triangular

dentate with sharp teeth projecting out about 90 degrees

determinate (of thorns) ceasing to grow longer after the first year of growth

diploid with a double set of chromosomes

distal away from the base

ellipsoidal elliptic, three dimensionally

elliptic a form with curved margins wherein the long axis is about 2–3 times as long as the short axis and the widest point is in the center of the axis

entire (of edges) without teeth or lobes; smooth

epetiolate without a leaf stalk

erose eroded (fruiting calyx lobes); with a cavity (nutlets)

exfoliating peeling off in thin flakes

frugivore an animal or bird that eats fruit

glabrescent starting hairy, becoming glabrous

glabrous without hair

gland a small, usually dotlike secretory organ

globose spherical

haw a hawthorn fruit, or colloquially, the whole plant

herbaceous (bracteole) of a somewhat leaflike character, more or less green, with evident venation

hypanthium in *Crataegus*, the tissue that encloses the carpels or nutlets and becomes the flesh of the fruit (see chapter 2 and plate 6)

impressed sunken in

indeterminate (of thorns) normally developing into a short shoot in a year or two

inferior (ovary) situated below the insertion of sepals, petals, and stamens

inflorescence an aggregation of flowers subtended by one true leaf

infructescence an aggregation of fruit subtended by one true leaf

lamina blade (of a leaf); see petiole

lanceolate a narrow shape, with the basal end widest and gradually tapering from there to the tip

leaf incision index (LII) depth to which a leaf is lobed; LII = 0 if no sinus; LII = 100 if sinus reaches midrib

lenticel a small, usually elliptic or round (usually less than 2 mm in diameter) corky area that assists in gaseous exchange and is found on fruit or young twigs

lobe a projecting part of the edge of a leaf usually more or less symmetric around a vein

mesophyte a plant that prefers a middling (neither wet nor dry) water regime

nutlet a hard, seedlike organ in fruit of hawthorns that is actually a bony carpel enclosing two tiny seeds

ob- generally refers to the same shape the opposite way up

oblong (leaf) with significant (at least one-third) proportion of sides of leaf more or less parallel

obovate egg-shaped; like an egg standing on its thin end

ovary female part of a flower

ovate egg-shaped

ovule a precursor of seed found in flowers; egg is fertilized inside ovule

panicle an inflorescence with a primary axis and at least secondary plus tertiary branching

pectinate deeply cut, like a comb

petal an usually delicate, colored organ that makes a flower conspicuous to pollinators (see plate 6)

petiole leaf stalk

pilose hairy

polyploid with more than two sets of chromosomes

pome a fruit type characteristic of Rosaceae subfamily Maloideae wherein carpels are invested by the fleshy hypanthium

precocious (of flowers) produced before much, or even any, leaf expansion

primary axis main or central axis

proximal end nearer to the base

pruinose with waxy covering (that generally grays or whitens the appearance)

pseudogamy apparent pollination (see chapter 2)

pubescent shortly and softly hairy

punctate dotted (dots are often lenticels)

pyrene technical term for nutlets

pyriform pear-shaped (widest end distal)

rhombic diamond-shaped (as in the "diamond" of playing cards); with leaves which will at best be only approximately rhombic—this, however, quite common in hawthorns

rugose with a wrinkled surface

scabrous rough-hairy

secondary axes (or veins) branching off the primary axis (or vein)

sepals green parts that completely cover the flower in bud (see plate 6)

serrate with forward-pointing teeth

sinus bay between two lobes (of a leaf)

spathulate salt-spoon-shaped

stamen male organ of flower, composed of filament (stalk) and anther

stigma a receptive surface for pollen; often a small knoblike structure at the end of the style

stipule small foliar appendage at the base of a leaf stalk; in hawthorns often falcate, toothed, and glandular

style a stalklike process which arises from the ovary and supports the stigma

sub- generally, equals less than; sometimes, equals below

subcordate not very strongly cordate

tetraploid with four sets of chromosomes (tetraploids are normally more or less fertile)

thorn a sharp element derived from a branch system, as in *Crataegus*

tomentose densely hairy

triploid with three sets of chromosomes (triploids are normally sterile)

truncate cut off at the base; in practice, the base of the leaf at right angles to the main axis and leaf stalk

venation the pattern of veins

villous somewhat long hairy

winged with flattened longitudinal processes; in hawthorns usually the thin strip of lamina along distal part of petiole

xeriscaping gardening without irrigation

xeromorphic adapted to survival in dry conditions

Bibliography

American Forestry Association Staff. 1999. *National Register of Big Trees*. Washington, D.C.: American Forestry Association.

Anonymous. 1890. *Crataegus grignonensis*. In *Illustrierte Gartenz*. Vienna.

Baird, J., and J. Thieret. 1989. The medlar (*Mespilus germanica*, Rosaceae) from antiquity to obscurity. *Economic Botany* 43: 328–372.

Bellair, G. 1899. Hybrides anormaux. *Rev. Hort.* 71: 482–484.

Bensky, D., and A. Gamble, compilers. 1993. *Chinese Herbal Medicine: Materia Medica*. Seattle: Eastland Press.

Boulger, G. S. 1907. *Familiar Trees*. London: Cassell.

Camp, W. H. 1942. The *Crataegus* problem. *Castanea* 7: 51–55.

Carrière, E. G. 1883. *Crataegus carrierei. Rev. Hort.* 55 (?): 108–109, and figure.

Chevalier, A. 1996. *Encyclopedia of Medicinal Plants*. London: Dorling Kindersley.

Chiej, R. 1984. *The Macdonald Encyclopedia of Medicinal Plants*. London: Macdonald.

Christensen, K. I. 1992. Revision of *Crataegus* section *Crataegus* in the Old World. *Systematic Botany Monographs* 35: 1–199. Ann Arbor, Michigan: ASPT.

Coleman, W. 1885. The medlar. *Garden* (London) 28: 473.

Craft, B. R., G. Melcher, and E. Langston. 1996. *Mayhaws: A Guide to Orchard Production and Propagation*. Kearney, Louisiana: Morris Publishing.

Dai, Yin-fang, and Cheng-jui Lui. 1982. *Fruit as Medicine*. Australia: Ram's Skull Press.

Dickinson, T. A., S. Belaousoff, R. M. Love, and M. Muniyamma. 1996. North American black-fruited hawthorns. I. *Folia Geobotanica Phytotaxonomica* 31: 355–371.

Dunning, R. 1976. *Christianity in Somerset*. Taunton: Somerset County Council.

130

Eggleston, W. W. 1909. The Crataegi of Mexico and Central America. *Bulletin of the Torrey Botanical Club* 36: 501–514.

Foreman, L., and D. Bridson. 1989. *The Herbarium Handbook*. Kew: Royal Botanic Gardens.

Franco, J. do O. 1968. *Crataegus*. In T. G. Tutin et al., eds., *Flora Europaea*, vol. 2. Cambridge: University Press.

Friend, H. 1884. *Flowers and Flower Lore*. London.

Geerinck, D. 1998. Considérations taxonomiques et nomenclaturelles sur quelques arbres cultivées en Europe: genres *Acer, Aesculus, Betula, Crataegus, Platanus, Prunus* et *Taxus*. *Belgique Journal de Botanique* 130: 119–130.

Gerard, J. 1597. *Herball*. London.

Gosler, A. G., C. K. Kelly, and J. K. Blakey. 1994. Phenotypic plasticity in leaf morphology of *Crataegus monogyna* (Rosaceae): an experimental study with taxonomic implications. *Journal of the Linnean Society, Botany* 115: 211–219.

Hillier, H. G. 1981. *Hillier's Manual of Trees and Shrubs*. 5th ed. Newton Abbot: David and Charles.

Hole, C. 1976. *British Folk Customs*. London: Hutchinson.

Knees, S. J., and M. C. Warwick. 1995. *Crataegus*. In J. Cullen et al., eds., *European Garden Flora*, vol. 4. Cambridge: University Press.

Kruschke, E. P. 1955. *Hawthorns of Wisconsin*. Milwaukee Public Museum Publ. Bot. 2: 1–124.

Lance, R. W. 1995. *Hawthorns of the Southeastern United States*. Fletcher, North Carolina: Author.

Lance, R. W., and J. B. Phipps. 2000. *Crataegus harbisonii*—rediscovery and amplification. *Castanea* 65: 291–296.

Launert, E. 1981. *Hamlyn Guide to Edible and Medicinal Plants*. London: Hamlyn.

Lavallée, A. 1880. *Crataegus lavallei*. In *Icones selectae arborum et fruticum*. Hortis Segrezianis collectorum. Part 1: 6–8, pl. 7. Paris: Baillière et fils.

Lawrence Review of Natural Products. January 1994. *Hawthorn*. St. Louis, Missouri.

Loudon, J. C. 1838. *Arboretum et Fruticetum Britanicum*. 2 vols. London: Longman.

Mabey, R. 1996. *Flora Britannica*. London: Sinclair Stevenson.

Moerman, D. E. 1998. *Native American Ethnobotany*. Portland, Oregon: Timber Press.

Moxham, R. 2000. *The Great Hedge of India*. London: Constable.

Newall, C. A., L. A. S. Anderson, and J. D. Phillipson. 1996. *Herbal Medicines*. London: Pharmaceutical Press.

Ody, P. 1993. *Complete Medicinal Herbal*. London: Dorling Kindersley.

Palmer, E. J. 1932. The *Crataegus* problem. *Journal of the Arnold Arboretum* 13: 342–362.

Palmer, E. J. 1950. *Crataegus*. In M. L. Fernald, *Gray's New Manual of Botany*, 8th ed. New York: American Book Company. 767–801.

Palmer, E. J. 1952. *Crataegus*. In H. A. Gleason, *New Britton and Brown Illustrated Flora of the Northeastern United States and Adjacent Canada*. New York: Haffner. 2: 338–375.

Pharmacopeia Commission of People's Republic of China. 1992. *Pharmacopeia of the Peoples' Republic of China*. Guangdong Science and Technical Press (translation of Chinese edition, 1990).

Phipps, J. B. 1990. *Mespilus canescens*, a new rosaceous endemic from Arkansas. *Systematic Botany* 15: 26–32.

Phipps, J. B. 1997. Monograph of northern Mexican *Crataegus* (Rosaceae, subfamily Maloideae). *SIDA, Botanical Miscellany* 15: 1–94.

Phipps, J. B., and R. J. O'Kennon. 1998. Three new species of *Crataegus* (Rosaceae) from western North America: *C. okennonii*, *C. okanaganensis*, and *C. phippsii*. *SIDA* 18: 169–181.

Phipps, J. B., and R. J. O'Kennon. 2002. New taxa of *Crataegus* from the northern Okanagan–southwestern Shuswap diversity center. *SIDA* 20: 115–144.

Phipps, J. B., K. R. Robertson, P. G. Smith, and J. R. Rohrer. 1990. A checklist of subfamily Maloideae (Rosaceae). *Canadian Journal of Botany* 68: 2209–2269.

Pojarkova, A. I. 1939. *Crataegus*. In V. L. Komarov and S. V. Juzepchuk, eds., *Flora of the USSR* (in Russian). 9: 416-468. Bot. Inst. Acad. Sci. USSR. English translation pp. 317–356. 1971 by Israel Program for Scientific Translation, Jerusalem.

Pollard, E., M. D. Hooper, and N. W. Moore. 1974. *Hedges*. New York: Taplinger.

Rackham, O. 1994. *The Illustrated History of the Countryside*. London: Phoenix Press.

Rehder, A. 1940. *Manual of Cultivated Trees and Shrubs*. 2nd ed. New York: Mac-Millan.

Reichenbach, L., and H. G. Reichenbach. 1903. *Icones florae Germanicae et Helveticae* 25 (16). Leipzig: Frederic Zezschwitz.

Reynolds, J. E. F. 1989. *Martindale, the Extra Pharmacopeia*. London: Pharmaceutical Press.

Rolland, E. 1904. *Flore Populaire*, vol. 4. Paris: Author.

Sargent, C. S. 1890. *Crataegus brachyacantha*. In *Silva of North America*. Cambridge, Massachusetts: Murray Printing Company. 4: 89.

Sargent, C. S. 1902. *Crataegus fecunda. Botanical Gazette* 33: 111.

Schweitzer, J. A., and K. C. Larson. 1999. Greater morphological plasticity of exotic honeysuckle species make them better invaders than native species. *Journal of the Torrey Botanical Society* 126: 15–23.

Seymour, F. C. 1982. *Crataegus.* In *Flora of New England*, 2nd ed. *Phytologia Memoirs* 5: 611.

Turner, W. 1562. *New Herball.* Part 2. London.

Vickery, R. A. 1979. *Holy Thorns of Glastonbury.* West Country Folklore, no. 12. St. Peter Port, Guernsey.

Vickery, R. A. 1995. *A Dictionary of Plant-Lore.* Oxford University Press.

Weir, A. 2001. *Henry VIII: The King and His Court.* New York: Ballantine Books.

Wickham, C. 1981. *Common Plants as Natural Remedies.* F. Mueller.

Wolton, R. 1999. Do we need hedges anymore? *Biologist* 46: 118–122.

Wurzell, B. 1992. Foreign *Crataegus* in Britain: a thorny problem. *Botanical Society of the British Isles News* 61: 42–45.

Young, J. A., and C. G. Young. 1992. *Seeds of Woody Plants in North America.* Portland Oregon: Dioscorides Press, an imprint of Timber Press.

Yü, T. T., and T. C. Ku. 1974. *Crataegus.* In T. T. Yü, ed., *Flora of the Peoples' Republic of China* (in Chinese) 36: 186–206. Beijing: Academia Sinica.

Index

Boldfaced numbers indicate main entries.